Why Women Buy

Why Women Buy

How to Sell to the World's Largest Market

By DAWN JONES with
Sherry Prindle

Made for Success
P.O. Box 1775
Issaquah, WA 98027

Why Women Buy: How to Sell to the World's Largest Market

Library of Congress Cataloging-in-Publication data

Jones, Dawn and Prindle, Sherry
Why Women Buy: How to Sell to the World's Largest Market
    p. cm.
ISBN: 978-1-61339-877-7 (pbk.)
LCCN: 2016911404

To contact the publisher, please email
service@MadeforSuccess.net or call +1 425 657 0300.

Printed in the United States of America

Praise for
Why Women Buy

"Having read many sales books during my career as a speaker/author, few books address the particular differences of selling to women. Dawn Jones brings poignant insights to reasons behind what motivates women to make buying decisions."

~Chris Widener, speaker and author
of *The Case for Network Marketing*

"This book just makes sense. The more we can understand about our buyers, the more we can grow as sales professionals. I highly recommend reading this book."

~Tom Hopkins, author of *How to Master
the Art of Selling and When Buyers Say "No"*

"*Why Women Buy* is a MUST HAVE for everyone in sales! Dawn artfully uncovers the subtle differences of how men and women arrive at their buying decisions. Understanding why women buy is the first step to gaining their business. This is especially important as they are the gateway to everybody else. This revelation alone provides a compelling reason to understand the impact of gender in the sales and marketing process."

~Cyndi O'Neill-Dady, Exceptional
Connections Networking CEO/Founder and
Relationships Marketing Strategist

"*Why Women Buy* is the 21st century game-changer in sales!"
~Meisha Rouser, Leadership and
Professional Development

"The buying market is always a challenge; however, Dawn shares insights to the person and their process. She breaks it down into easy to understand categories from her experiences and facts that will enhance your selling process."
~Jeff Wagoner, International Consultant
and author of *Discover the Unseen*

"When I started reading this book I was immediately hooked! The stories and research taught me about my own thought process. Would recommend to friends!"
~Anna Magidson, Ski Instructor
at Snow Sports Northwest

"As a professional speaker/author who negotiates with women, *Why Women Buy* will be my go-to-guide for years to come."
~Cara Lane, International speaker and
author of *Assertiveness Training*

"Being an entrepreneur for over 25-years, *Why Women Buy* and Dawn Jones have significantly changed my approach and increased my sales when selling to women."
~Lara Lambert, Owner, Northwestern
Fuels and Super Cedar FireStarters

Contents

Preface

Over the past 25 years I've discovered some powerful and effective sales techniques that work; techniques that have been implemented by great salespeople across the span of time. These techniques have are detailed in many books-but *inadvertently geared towards selling to men.* This sales book is different because it is intentionally geared towards selling to women.

When selling to women, there are subtle yet major differences. Many of these differences are hidden in plain sight and, once discovered, can make all the difference in the sales outcome. I call these hidden techniques *secrets* for two reasons. First, as a woman who buys things, I thought there needed to be a book that reveals these techniques in order to help salespeople specifically and effectively sell to women. Second, after years of studying and implementing traditional sales techniques, I wished someone had shared this wisdom with me earlier in my career—especially when selling to women.

With years of professional sales, international speaking, and the privilege of being a best-selling author, I have made a career of studying and implementing these techniques and turning them into intentional techniques that have been consolidated into this book. During our time together, I'll be sharing with you these techniques for selling to women so that you too can be more intentional and effective in your sales career.

Some of the concepts that I give you can be applied to both men and women. In this program, though, I'm focusing on the subtle variances that make all the difference in the sales process when your client is a woman.

I have also invited input and content from my colleague and friend, Sherry Prindle. Sherry is an outstanding Master Coach, international speaker, and corporate trainer. She has delivered over four thousand programs covering sixty topics in three languages. She founded the Professional Coach Academy and hosts a weekly radio show. Here's a note from Sherry:

I specialize in behavioral issues and how they affect real-world performance. Dawn brings the experience, the stories, the insights, and step-by-step solutions; while I bring research, structure, and explanation. Through the combination of our specializations and backgrounds, we have created for you a relevant resource that will improve your sales results while allowing you to meet the needs of this powerful force in the marketplace.

Introduction

This is it, a meeting with a huge prospective client. You reviewed the research and rehearsed presenting why you are the best choice to serve the client's needs. Your slides include the client's logo and pictures of their facility. You address every concern from the client's Request for Proposal. The presentation is nearly flawless, but you feel like you are never quite on the same wavelength with the client representatives. What could explain the lack of rapport in the room?

When this scenario actually happened to seven partners and senior staffers at Deloitte Consulting, the deciding factor was that half the client attendees were women. The consultants had known this would be the case ahead of time, but it hadn't occurred to them to alter their pitch in any way and, as a result, Deloitte did not get the job.

Multiple studies have found that women are more likely to prepare conscientiously for meetings. Women directors also frequently ask questions, so decisions are less likely to be nodded through. Women also become more vocal and active when there are three or more females present.[1]

Also, be aware that women are more likely than men to see things through a gendered lens; bringing to new interactions their accumulated experience of dealing professionally, academically, and personally with men. Their antennae are particularly raised toward anything that smacks of male condescension.[2]

By picking up this book, you are tapping into the power to serve a largely ignored segment of the population, a group with around $7 trillion in buying power that within the next decade will control two-thirds of consumer wealth.

According to research compiled by The Terri and Sandy Solution, women are responsible for 85 percent of all consumer purchases, including over 50 percent of traditional male products. At the same time, 91 percent of women say that advertisers "don't understand them."[3]

While women have been around all along, marketers, salespeople, and service providers have only recently begun to recognize the benefits of adapting to them.

The Bureau of Labor Statistics shows that women hold half of all managerial and professional positions in the United States and make up 41 percent of employees with authority to make buying decisions.

Have you ever found yourself in a similar sales situation to Deloitte Consulting, where something just wasn't right? Perhaps the rapport wasn't quite there; you felt out of sync, or you got some unexpected questions you weren't sure you answered effectively. Do you even know what happened? Do you have any idea what you could have done differently to make the sale? The challenge is how you recover from or, better yet, prepare for these types of encounters with women— without coming across as insincere, weak, incompetent or condescending.

As you read this book, these issues and much more will be addressed. By the time you're finished, you will have the confidence to immediately apply what you've learned, along with the ability to more effectively sell to women. These techniques are your keys to success when selling to women. Here is a brief overview of each chapter and what you can expect to learn.

Chapter 1 — Recognize How Women Differ from Men examines scientific research on gender differences and gives you specific strategies for targeting women.

Chapter 2 — Overcome the Fear of Sales gives you the motivation to go after the sale and have confidence when selling to women.

Chapter 3 — Operate with Integrity is the foundation for your sales process particularly with women.

Chapter 4 — Ask Great Questions uncovers principles of influence that open doors, almost magically, to selling to women.

Chapter 5 — Integrate All Four Communication Styles is the key to engagement, understanding, and effectively conveying your sales message.

Chapter 6 — Sell to the Different Personality Types provides you the power of rapport.

Chapter 7 — The Four Stages of Competency builds an action plan for you so that you can achieve long-term success in selling to women.

My goal in sharing the techniques for selling to women is to help you be more intentional and effective in your sales process with women while operating with the highest degree of integrity. When you are more cognizant of your thoughts and intentions towards women, you will be better prepared to handle obstacles and overcome objections that arise throughout the sales process.

Chapter 1

Recognize How Women
Differ from Men

Consumer trend expert, Faith Popcorn, says, "Companies think they're marketing to women, but they're not. They're not talking to women. They don't know how to talk to women. They really don't realize that women have a separate language and a separate way of being."[4]

This is a departure from the recent tendency to try and gender-neutralize everything. So, to be clear, my goal here is to recognize gender-specific tendencies, not stereotypes.

A *TIME Magazine* cover article from January of 1992 said, "It has been proven scientifically that men and women are different."[5] If you grew up before 1992, you already knew this, but now it is official.

I discovered those sales differences on a beautiful Pacific Northwest day one summer when my husband and I decided to make a major purchase. A boat. Not just a little boat, but one big enough for us to live aboard.

While many people dream of buying their first home, my lifelong dream had been to buy and live on a boat. For me, it was an adventure to have a season in my life that romantic songs are written about and wanderlust artists put to canvas. Whether walking through a marina at sunrise and watching the boats make ready to embark on their journeys or winding down in the cool of the evening after a day at sea, with the gentle lapping of water alongside a resting boat; life on the water called to me.

Though I dreamed about this for years, it wasn't until I had written it down as one of my goals in my success journal, and then shared that dream with my husband, that this goal turned into a reality. Based on the direction we were going in our lives at that time, this was a practical decision as well as an adventure.

There was one slight problem. Due to our current circumstances, my husband would not be present when I looked for and purchased the boat. For several weeks, I called and visited numerous yacht brokers. Every time a salesperson found out I was married and my husband would not be present in the decision-making process, they immediately stopped taking me seriously as a prospective buyer. I mean, after all, who would take a 20-something married woman serious about a major purchase like a big boat *without her husband being present?*

Thankfully, I was determined (and naïve enough) to not let that deter me. Determined in the sense that this decision was a done deal—we just needed to find the right boat. Naïve in the sense that I didn't notice

I was being brushed aside in the sales process. Until I met Chet.

Chet looked as though he had spent many years enjoying a lifestyle of boating. He was well-dressed, yet casual. He was rugged but had gentle eyes. I still remember the sweet smell that wafted from his tobacco pipe—it reminded me of a faint, yet comforting, childhood memory.

It must have been a slow sales day because Chet took the time to show me a few boats. In the process, he *listened* to what I told him my husband and I were looking for and accepted me not disclosing the reasons for the lack of his presence. I think he was intrigued because he continued to work with me—and in a very professional manner.

After many weeks, and several trips to different marinas, I asked Chet why he took me seriously while the other yacht brokers I had visited hadn't. This was when I was enlightened. Chet let me in on a little-known secret in the yacht world. He told me that while women were definitely influential on the buying decision of a boat, it was usually about the interior and the comfort— how it looked and felt—but ultimately the final buying decision rested on the man. Single men bought boats. Married men bought boats (even without their wives being present). On rare occasion single women bought boats. But it was unheard of for a married woman to buy a big boat without her husband!

Chet was always professional, never condescending, and had a high degree of integrity. He asked great questions that he wove naturally into our conversations.

He listened to my answers then went about looking for, and ultimately finding, our perfect boat.

Though I purchased alone, Chet got *our* business. My husband and I lived in our boat on Seattle's Lake Union for two and one-half years.

The following chapters reveal the techniques—the art and science—that great salespeople like Chet apply to their work and lives beginning with the real differences between men and women.

There are quite a few physical differences between male and female brains that explain how women process information. An actual look at the process of how the electrical neurons fire back and forth in the brain brings some interesting conclusions.

First of all, men form a linear point from the back of their brains to the front of their brains. Anything that interferes with them taking that thought, process or action from the back of their brain to the front is treated as an obstacle. Men will push that obstacle out of their way whether it's from the back to the front or the front to the back. New concepts run on a linear line, kind of like a football field. This is a perfect analogy of how a man's brain works; they run back and forth until they score points to win the game.

While there are a lot of women who are sports fans, for a woman, her thought process is more than just running a linear path. Using the same football analogy, it's more of a zig-zag that includes a very different pre-game, game, and post-game. It's making sure life is in place before the game begins; food is purchased and prepared, interruptions are minimized, and TV commercials are optimized. Then, once the game is over women are generally not talking about the instant replays or statistics of the players or even about winning and conquest and scoring points. What do you think they're more likely talking about? Relationships. Women tend to talk and think more about the fairness of a sports play, the dynamics of the players, or even how the win or loss will affect their family, friends, and co-workers. On a side-note, apparently Super Bowl fans on the winning team have more babies nine months after the win—now how's that for relational! So how do these brain differences impact relationships in the workplace? While women are thinking "How can we advance in the workplace?" It's totally different. They are also thinking "How do we get along?" They are thinking about *their* advancement *and* the impact on their relationships as they advance.

While men's thoughts move between the front and back of their brains, women's thoughts tend to go side—to-side from one hemisphere to the other, from the right brain to left brain, left brain to right brain. What is the difference between the right and left sides of the brain? There's an easy way I can help you remember.

The left side of the brain tends to be logical, sequential, and linear. I put lots of L's in there to help you remember. This is the most logical path. This is the infrastructure. This is the scaffolding. You want to use this side of the brain when you're talking to people who are direct personality types, or thinker-analyzer personality types (we'll cover more on how to talk with differing personalities in a later chapter). Bottom line— the left brain is logical, sequential, and linear.

The right side of the brain is relational, random, responsive, and reactive; it is more creative. You want to use this side of the brain when you're talking to social extroverts and relational personality types.

Women are said to be more right-brained and more relational. When I read the popular book *Men Are from Mars; Women Are from Venus* I felt like the author, John Gray, described the difference between males and females in a way I recognized as whether the right or left brain was dominant—which is an oversimplification. The reality is that women have a greater ability to jump back and forth between logical computations or processing facts in the left hemisphere, and emotional processing of visual imagery or interpreting context in the right.

Here's a bit of the science to support that. According to a study conducted at the University of California, Irvine, men's brains have approximately 6.5 times more gray matter than women's, and women's brains have nearly 10 times more white matter than men's. Because gray matter characterizes information processing centers and white matter facilitates the connections among those centers, scientists theorize that those differences might explain why men tend to excel in tasks that depend on sheer processing while women show relative strength in tasks that call for assimilating and integrating disparate pieces of information. What's more, the corpus callosum, which is the bridge of nerve tissue that connects the left and right lobes, is 10% thicker, on average, in female brains.[6] So, basically, women use both sides of their brains to solve problems, while men predominantly use the left side of their brains.

This explains why women and men can get frustrated when talking to each other. Sally and Bennett Shaywitz of Yale University gave men and women a rhyming task while taking an MRI. The results showed that in men, a small center of the brain lit up only on the left side. When women performed the same activity, the brain looked more like a pinball machine, with multiple sites lighting up on both sides. Perhaps this drives males to think females are "all over the map."[7]

You might be wondering what this has to do with you and your sales process. Here's the relevance of this secret, if you're speaking to a man he wants the facts. He wants to stay on course. He wants to go up or down the left or right but not zigzag between them. If you are selling to a woman, you will need to switch back and forth between the logic and emotion, and it can happen in a snap or even all at once.

But what is the reason for the difference? About 2,500 years ago Aristotle had this to say about the female brain, "The female is softer in disposition, is more mischievous, less simple, more impulsive and more attentive to the nurture of the young... the fact is, the nature of man is the most rounded off and complete."

Does this historical philosophy actually support the new research about gender differences? Let's take a look at a few more historical standards and expectations for both males and females. Little girls and boys are raised with certain expectations, and I'll bet you're pre-programmed with some cultural expectations. Many little boys grew up with slugs and snails and...yes, puppy dog's tails. Little girls were reminded to be sugar and spice and...all things nice. Little boys were encouraged to go out and play and win and be competitive and expected to get themselves dirty. Little girls were supposed to go outside to play and play nice—and to make sure they were not going to get dirty. Yeah, that's a clean dress! These were things that boys and girls grew up with.

While those are your typical stereotypes, interestingly, Diane Carlson Jones has found that a "key difference between boys and girls is the perception of power holders. Boys readily accept the occupants of top-ranking positions, while girls reject the powerful...only the indirect power style is socially sanctioned; the aggressive style is increasingly closed off as an option."[8]

What this means is that even though boys and girls are raised with cultural expectations, they are also more inclined to instinctively act certain ways, in part, to the way each is wired differently. Take, for example, if a little boy got into a fight at school. When he came home, he'd usually get in trouble for it and Mom would say something like, "You shouldn't have done that. That was not very nice of you; don't you know better than that?" Generally speaking, mom wants to instill that "You've got to be a good citizen and play nice" type of influence.

Many research studies have shown that children have definite ideas about how powerful males and females "should" be and also who "should" control interactions between them. In one study, children as young as two or three already understood that "girls don't hit, but boys like to fight."[9]

Women are naturally encoded to have a tender, softer side. Of course, some women have grown up in environments where they had to, or wanted to, be tougher; or where the softer, feminine side was not encouraged or modeled. Still, science shows the females of every species are wired to be more nurturing or maternal than males. If there is still any doubt about this fact, visit a local dairy farm and watch the nurturing that takes place between the mother cow and her calf. Or watch a video clip of a cat with her new kittens or dog with her new puppies or a mother with her newborn baby. The evidence is overwhelming. This is not to say that women are *less than* or that these traits are to be viewed as weaknesses, it is quite the opposite. These are positive characteristics of women that help keep the balance in a civilized world.

Men, on the other hand, may have a different approach to talking about the school fight. The dad might openly say something disapproving to the son yet secretly when no one is looking, he might ask, "Okay, son, who won?" because, remember, by a man's standard that's the objective. In addition to winning, men are wired to instinctively want to protect and defend the weak or vulnerable by fighting and eliminating the enemy—that *John Wayne* kind of protection. Granted, that type of chivalry spawned a huge demand for modern-day video games where it's all about conquest and winning. (If there's any doubt, research annual video game sales to boys and young men.) Though, having said that, I believe chivalry is not dead, and I'm glad there are many men and women who are committed to keeping it alive. Recognize, though, some men have grown up in environments where they had to, or wanted to, be more tender or the masculine side was not encouraged or modeled. The facts still remain; science shows men are wired differently and tend to be bigger, stronger, and faster than women and, as mentioned earlier, even our brains process information differently.

We've covered the physical and cultural differences between men and women beginning with when they are boys and girls; let's move now to the more subtle differences including the emotional and relational aspects.

When you're talking to a woman in the selling process, remember there is a relational aspect, even if you're asking her questions. She wants to know at the very beginning of that process that your questions are genuine—I'll cover in more detail the types of questions to ask her in the *Ask Great Questions* chapter of this book. She wants to know that you are real, sincere, and unpretentious. She wants to know you're going to ask questions that are relevant to her. She wants to know that you care about her.

Clinical Psychologist Susan Heitler, Ph.D., explains, "When women face a decision, they tend to begin by collecting data. They do this by asking others' thoughts on a question. When men hear these questions, they think they are being asked for a plan of action. If the woman thinks further about other factors and decides against the man's plan, whoops, the man feels his idea was rejected."[10]

The reason women don't implement the initial plan of action that's been presented to them is because women don't allow themselves to fail the same way men allow themselves to fail. Metaphorically speaking, women want to have all their ducks in a row before they cross the street. Therefore, they need to run that action plan through the zig-zag pattern in their brain to see how it will play out. Also, realize when you're selling to women that they do not like to fail in their purchasing decisions. While men don't like to fail either, men *do* fail more because they risk more. They also succeed more because they risk more. Women, however, fail less because they risk less. Like men, women don't like to lose—the secret here though is not so much for the reason of competition. It's because it affects their whole being. For many women, who they are is a part of what they do and if their work is rejected, it's a reflection on them; they are being rejected, not just their work. Whereas the way a man's brain is wired allows many men to separate the right brain emotion of who they are from the left brain logic of what they do for work—they are more able to compartmentalize and keep it from being personal.

Keep those aspects in mind when presenting your sales presentation to a woman. Realize you must be genuine if you want to make this a win-win for her, not just on a superficial level but at a deep interwoven relational *and* logical level. With that in mind, remember to be sincere *and* prepared *and* ready to switch gears when selling to women.

There are three steps to having a win-win encounter with women. The first and last steps come rather naturally to both genders; it is the middle step you cannot afford to skip when selling to women.

Step One: Offer an initial solution idea
Step Two: Explore underlying concerns
Step Three: Decide on a plan of action

The tendency to jump from idea to plan of action makes sense based on research from the University of Warwick that suggests men and women see the world differently. Their study proved that men tend to organize the world into distinct categories while women see shades of gray. Be careful, as these descriptions oversimplify gender differences and make them seem extreme, but "small but consistent" differences between males and females show men to be more comfortable in the black-and-white world of categorical thinking as women operate more within the world of context.

When listening to a sales presentation, men want just facts and figures, without the *fluff,* and are often more focused on what they're getting for the best price. Women want the complete story and are more interested in learning about quality and getting the right product or service to suit their needs.

At work, women see a big meeting with a potential service provider as a chance to explore options in collaboration with an expert resource, while men see that event as a near-final step in the process. Men tend to end a conversation once they connect with a good idea or solution while women are inclined to be more inquisitive, wanting to hear everyone's thoughts before deciding.

By the way, traditional male buyers want the buyer's power over the seller to be acknowledged. Thus, high-ranking people from the seller organization make appearances at meetings to signal the importance of the project. Women are less likely to see the value of such rituals. It's more important to female buyers to meet the people they will be working with.[11]

Dr. Heitler suggests making sure you have satisfied a woman's need to explore by finishing with a good catch-all question like, "Are there any little pieces of this that still feel unfinished?" If you were to ask a man that question, he would look at you oddly; but by asking those types of questions to women, you ensure that you address that second, often times overlooked, step and explore her underlying concerns—the key step in effectively selling to women. Only then can you move onto the third step of deciding a plan of action.

Bottom line. This is one of those secrets that is hidden in plain sight and tends to be minimized or overlooked during the sales process. Allow these differences into your sales process. Acknowledge and accentuate the positive differences as outlined in this chapter and you will be well on your way to creating a win-win situation.

Chapter 2

Overcome the Fear of Sales

This is one of my favorite topics because I used to be terrified of certain aspects of the sales process, such as making sales calls. I would have rather had a wasp fly into my car while I was driving down the highway than pick up the phone or walk into an office and make a sales call to some unknown organization—the dreaded *cold call*. Though I was an able salesperson, I was afraid to pick up the phone and make a simple call.

I would become paralyzed by the thought. My voice would quiver. My hands would get cold. I would think of every possible distraction. Can I go eat something? Can I do some laundry? Can I go to the dentist? I found myself looking for any distraction, rather than making a phone call. Have you ever found yourself in that type of situation?

Think about it. You may have more talent than somebody who's actually making a living doing what you want to do, but if you have practiced allowing the pain of fear to paralyze you and your sales efforts like I did, then it's time to replace those old bad habits with some new great habits.

While this chapter is geared towards the techniques for overcoming the fear of sales, it is as much about *you* as well as who you are selling to. Two things to keep in mind when selling to women are to remember that women *don't* like to risk if they think they're going to fail, and they *do* like you to engage them with relevant questions. Regarding women and failing, I am reminded of something that I've never forgotten my younger brother saying to me when we were children. He said, "Dawn, it's not what's on the outside that blocks you, it's what's on the inside that holds you back." That is a great explanation of a reaction to irrational fear—and if a woman has an irrational fear that leads her to think she will fail, she won't take the risk. The same thing goes for a salesperson who has practiced being held back by fear while in the sales process.

Think about it. How many possibilities in life are you missing out on because you're afraid they might not turn out the way you hope? How many questions go unasked because you're afraid you might look incompetent, inept, or even stupid? How many potential sales calls do you not return because you talk yourself out of doing it, thinking they're not going to buy from you anyway? Yes, you heard me right; I said you talk yourself out of doing it! Fear is a bit like Murphy's Law, if you think about it long enough and rehearse it in your mind enough times, it's bound to happen.

Fear is instinctive, but your response to fear is *practiced* behavior. Yes, there is *fight or flight,* but there is also what I call *fight, flight, or deer in the headlights.* If your reaction to fear is to fight when faced with a threatening situation, you are wired instinctively to react to that threat by standing your ground and fighting. On the other hand, if your instinct is to run, you'll be looking for the closest exit and flying out of there!

Though fight or flight instinct is wired into all animals, one of the things that make humans different is the ability to be rational and reasonable; to think things through, come to a conclusion, make a decision, and take action. This is where the *practiced* behavior comes in. If you think through and practice how you'll react to a situation, you have a better chance of a positive outcome—similar to when you were a child practicing looking both ways before crossing the street. Contrast that with *not* practicing in advance, hoping you'll come up with something, and instead ending up standing there not knowing what to do—similar to a deer in the headlights of an oncoming car. If things aren't planned and practiced in advance, it is easy to become paralyzed by fear, unable to think of what to do next and then get knocked out of your element. Deer in the headlights occurs in sales when you are faced with a threatening situation, you dismiss your instinct, your logic takes over, and you don't have a plan—therefore you fail and reinforce the fear of never wanting to face that situation again in the future. Fear of failure in sales is practiced behavior.

The good news is that because you *do* have the ability to be rational and reasonable, you also have the ability to identify your fears in advance, think through your options, decide on your best option and then take action.

I want you to take a moment right now and imagine that you are about to pick up the phone and call a woman who might need what you're selling. You've never spoken to her before, and you've been told that she *hates* dealing with sales people. Stop for a moment and really think about this scenario. What thoughts are going through your head? What's physiologically happening to you? What instincts are kicking in for you? What patterns have you followed in the past?

When it comes to overcoming the fear of sales and replacing the old unproductive patterns of the past with new productive ones, there are three important elements.

1. **Know-how**: Knowing how to sell successfully.
2. **Leverage**: Leverage is something that propels you beyond your fear.
3. **Vision**: Vision is what motivates you to take action even when you don't feel like it.

Let's begin with the first element, Know-how. This will reduce your fear significantly, so you don't have to reinvent the wheel. How do you successfully sell? Success in sales leaves clues. Learn from somebody who has done what you want to do and as Nike® says, "*Just Do It.*"

It has been said that if you do what you fear most, the death of fear is certain. Even though this is true, in order to be able to do what you fear most, you must know *how* to do it successfully. Otherwise, as you know, you'll keep repeating the same mistakes over and over again and drive yourself crazy. That is the humorous definition of insanity, doing the same things over and over expecting different results. You see, what you practice is what you repeat.

Just like when you are learning something new, you practice repeatedly until what you've learned becomes natural and you can say or do it with little or no thought. This is the power of repetition. It is also the danger. You see, you have become who you are through a series of practiced habits. You consciously continue these habits until you have said or done something enough times that you are able to say or do it reactively or without thinking. Let me prove it to you right now. You may have heard an expression that starts out, "Practice makes..." what? Fill in the blank. Did you say "perfect"? If you really think about it, you know as well as I do, that is not always true. Practice does not make perfect. Practice makes permanent.

I'll prove it to you. Have you ever seen somebody on one of those television talent shows who gets up and thinks they can sing, but they can't? Who told them they could sing? The probability is they practiced for a very long time doing something poorly and those closest to them in life encouraged them to continue to *practice*. Unfortunately, practice did not make perfect; practice made *permanent*. Think about it, when we practice something we fall down, we make mistakes, and we learn what does and doesn't work; all the while hopefully still striving for improvement. The problem is, if we keep trying to fix ourselves without any outside help we'll continue to reinforce bad habits that we can't see, thus reinforcing the myth that practice makes perfect. The truth is that practice makes *permanent*.

Even as you just read those words, your brain might still be thinking *perfect*, because your brain has been in the habit of saying it that way for years. Yet, because we just talked about this concept, you probably slowed down and maybe caught yourself and said practice makes *permanent*. The same applies whether you're making cold calls, speaking, or selling to women. It's no different. Whatever you practice, the daily actions will be ingrained in your mind until they eventually become habits, good or bad.

Once a habit is established, you can't stop it; you can only replace it. If you're in the habit of being afraid to make sales calls, then it doesn't matter how much talent you have. Fear is fear. Moreover, if practiced continually, the habitual fear becomes an obstacle that can block you and hold you back from taking your talent out to the world. The good news is this obstacle can be removed. You do this by replacing the old, unproductive habit with a new, helpful habit. This is why understanding *how* to do something successfully and consistently is so important.

By creating a new way of doing something, that's different from the way you've been doing it; you're forming a habit that's duplicable. You can repeat the method because you understand how to do it. In this case, to become really good at selling, learn from somebody who does it successfully and copy them until it is second nature to you (which, by the way, is what you are doing right now). Then, take daily steps to ingrain that method into your brain so that it becomes a habit. A new habit that eventually becomes stronger than the old habit. This new habit gradually replaces the old habit and becomes a powerful yet natural part of your life.

The second element is leverage. Leverage is anything that compels you to take action. Leverage can be summed up with an expression you may have heard somewhere in your life, "No great change comes without pain." It's true. When the pain of not changing becomes greater than the pain of changing, we take action. When we are finally fed up with the obstacles that block us, we look for a new path to travel then take that journey. Now that is leverage in action.

Internationally famous motivational speaker, Anthony Robbins, has a very effective tool for getting leverage over yourself. He calls it the Dickens Pattern. Charles Dickens' *A Christmas Carol* character, Ebenezer Scrooge, is visited by the ghosts of Christmas past, present, and future. Likewise, think about your fear of sales or any other habit that has been holding you back. Consider all the pain it has caused you in the past—really experience it. Then think of the things it is keeping you from being able to do, be, and have in the present. Finish with a truthful look at how your future will look if you continue the way you are for a year...five years...ten years...twenty.

The idea is to create a scenario where the pain of staying the same exceeds the pain you've associated with selling, or cold-calling, or public speaking, or any habit where you've practiced fear in your mind and through your actions. This is no different than being at a swimming pool and standing on a high diving board for the first time with all the people waiting at the bottom of the ladder shouting, "Jump! Just jump into the water!" and finally, the pressure at the bottom of the ladder of being embarrassed in front of all of your friends exceeds the fear of jumping from the top of the diving board and you jump! When I'm coaching clients, and they face a fear, I will often times ask them "What's it going to take for you to jump?" We explore their options, come up with a viable solution, and then they jump! Another way to do this is to truly think about how what you sell will benefit the client. Realistically remind yourself that you would be doing her a disservice *not* to offer it to her. Read Chapter 7 for greater insights on how to turn your new thought pattern into a habit.

The third element in overcoming the fear of sales is vision. Have you ever been to a conference or an event, or watched a speaker or salesperson do something that you could do. Perhaps you thought to yourself, "I can do that," or "I want to do what he's doing," or maybe you thought, "She makes it look so easy. I want to be able to do that, too." One of my favorite proverbs says, "My people perish for lack of vision." Vision allows you to look beyond your current circumstances. It keeps the destination of your journey in front of you. Vision is seeing your goal or your dream in your mind as if it is completed. Vision reminds you of your purpose. Vision turns roadblocks into building blocks.

So what is your vision? What is your purpose? Remind yourself right now why you believe in the product or the service you are selling. Why do you believe women need what you have? Can you picture yourself in that sales call or in that sales presentation? You're delivering your message, and you're actually fulfilling your purpose while helping women fulfill a need or overcome an obstacle in their lives.

Think about your purpose. Can you define it? Can you envision it? Can you see how moving through some areas of fear and asking yourself, "*what's it going to take for me to jump?*" can help you overcome your obstacles, reach your vision, and live your life on purpose? Yes, it's a risk for you—is it worth the risk? When you look ahead ten years in your life and pretend you're looking back to where you are right now—what would you say to yourself? Would you say, "I wish I would have risked more to become more competent in the areas of life that could have given me such joy, fulfillment, and purpose"? Or would you say, "Good job, I took healthy risks. I became competent in areas I'd struggled with for years and now my life has more joy, fulfillment, and purpose." Remember your vision. When you place your vision in front of the obstacles in life, those obstacles will shrivel.

Scope out your vision on multiple levels. Start with the big picture. Your ideal life. Where would you like to be? What would you like to do and have? Consider all the areas of your life: career, finances, relationships, health, happiness, and spirituality. Next, connect the areas by asking yourself how each one affects the others. This builds a web of motivation.

Next, envision what it will take to get there. How much money would you like to earn? Whose attention do you have to get? How many calls do you need to make? What percent will you close? Whatever the measures are, consider them—then visualize. You have met the quota or surpassed your personal best. How do you feel? What do you see? What do you hear? The more sensory detail you provide, the more tangible it becomes. Visualize both these tangible and the big-picture outcomes on a regular basis to leverage your thoughts and feelings and align your subconscious with your goals. Vision goes beyond making money or creating a good name for yourself. Vision completes your destiny.

When helping your female client scope out her vision, realize that in the sales process, especially major sales decisions, you are leading her through some areas of fear. Remind yourself that it's not what's on the outside that's blocking her, it's what's inside that's holding her back. Know-how, leverage, and vision will help you assist her in identifying what she needs. Offering an initial solution, exploring underlying concerns, and helping her decide on a plan of action helps her to take that jump. It's a risk for her. She needs to know that there is a process where she can come out triumphant on the other side. Give her that vision.

Finally, before every encounter, envision a positive result. See the client smiling. Imagine shaking hands and signing the contract. Picture applause from the crowd or a pat on the back from your boss. Envision whatever symbolizes for you that you have pulled it off. Set yourself up for success on all levels.

Bottom line. As I stated at the beginning of this chapter, overcoming fear is just as much about you facing your fears as it is helping your clients face theirs. It is listed here in chapter two because in order to implement the other techniques into your life, you must do what you fear most to ensure the death of fear. This chapter has been designed to help you unravel the mystery of the fears that are holding you back and boil it down to know-how, leverage, and vision. You can then effectively use the same process with your female clients.

Chapter 3

Operate with Integrity

Perhaps you have heard somewhere in life, "Watch your thoughts; they become your words. Watch your words; they become your actions. Watch your actions; they become your habits or behaviors. Watch your habits and behaviors because they become your character, and watch your character because it's who you've become."

Most people may not be experts on human psychology, but they are experts on human behavior, and they know when they're being "sold" just like you know when you're being sold. What I don't want to do here is deter you from having a plan or using techniques while you are selling. Both are critical, and I'll briefly go over those aspects in just a moment. The main part of this practice that I want you to take away is that the level of integrity you bring to the conversation will determine the success of utilizing those techniques.

While integrity during the sales process is important to both men and women, if it is in question it tends to be more of a deal-breaker for women than men. Because men's minds are wired to focus more on the goal or the prize, they can put their ego in their back pocket and view the lack of integrity of the salesperson as just an obstacle in their path towards the finish line. If a man knows he's getting what he wants, he'll often overlook the process to get it. As long as he crosses the finish line with his prize in hand, he has won. Contrast that with a woman in the same situation.

If a woman believes the salesperson she is working with is disingenuous, she is more inclined to stop the sales process and *leave without her prize*. This can happen in several ways. She might bring the conversation to a close by saying she's not interested at this time. Or she could say that she'll have to come back later. She might even flat out ask for another salesperson or the sales manager. You might be asking yourself *why?* Why can't she just ignore the salesperson, buy what she wants and leave? This goes back to my earlier comments that women are involved on a more emotional level. There are some women who will just buy what they want and leave—though, when they tell you about their experience, they'll relive every painful part of the process (just like re-watching a bad movie); conveying every miserable detail of what the salesperson did or didn't do and how she had to put up with them and couldn't wait to get out of there! The problem with this scenario is that this woman relives her sales process from a grumbling and complaining perspective. For most women, the sales process is more than a transaction, depending on the product or service, whether cars, computers or cosmetics, it's an *experience*. The bigger the ticket price, the bigger the experience she wants to enjoy—to relive those memorable moments like watching a favorite movie; she wants to savor that enjoyment and tell her friends about it. Anything that interferes with her experience spoils the movie. Which explains why she'd rather leave that metaphoric movie rather than put up with the games of an insincere or incompetent salesperson during *her* sales experience. A woman's expectation of experiential service has an impact in retail stores and in the workplace.

Male directors with the experience of working with women directors even say that men's political behavior is tempered when women are present, partly because women want to get on with the task at hand rather than "play games." Male directors say that in the presence of women directors, men change their language, become more civilized, and moderate their masculinity. In their view, this led to more effective performance and better governance.[12]

When you bring a high degree of integrity to a woman, she's more inclined to listen to what you have to say because she believes you. The following question will help you examine your level of integrity. That question is: are you the same person publicly, privately, and secretly? What I mean by this question is, are you the same person when you are selling to your prospective customers as you are when you are talking about them privately behind their backs, or when nobody is watching or listening? The real measure of integrity is when all three of those line-up.

What about when you're not selling? Are you a person of integrity in your personal relationships? Do you have integrity even when you don't get the sale or get your way?

As a frequent flyer, I have traveled on many different airlines and have a few favorites. My preferred international carrier is Qantas because they go out of their way to provide the highest quality flying experience possible—both in comfort and safety. On a recent jam-packed trip, I was flying to a different city every night—Sydney, Brisbane, Melbourne, and Perth—and I was delivering seminars to groups ranging from 80—200 people each day. While in Australia, I was representing a client from the USA, who, as part of some budget cuts, stopped hiring chauffeured cars for their speakers, having us use taxis instead. Now you might be thinking, "Well, that makes sense, Dawn, because chauffeurs are a bit extravagant and aren't taxis more affordable? And don't you want to save your client money?" My answers are, "sometimes" and "yes." Sometimes taxis are more affordable and yes, saving my client money is important to me. As for the extravagance, let's compare apples to apples. Chauffeur drivers get paid by the job, whereas taxi drivers get paid by the time and distance.

Incidentally, my way of looking at the transportation options was consistent with the way women assess situations, and my client's viewpoint was consistent with that of a man, based on research at the University of Warwick. Psychologists found men were likely to engage in abstract thinking using categories, and generalizations, while women were more disposed to context-specific thinking—in terms of concrete situations and relationships. This is evident, for one thing, in how some psychologists contrast the moral reasoning of males and females. Males' moral judgments tend to be governed by abstract principles of justice, duty, and fairness that apply to all people and situations (in this case, going all or nothing in deciding to use taxis). A females' moral judgment tends to give more weight to specific relationships between people and extenuating circumstances in a given situation. Moral judgments are made through subjective feelings rather than abstract principles (recognizing there are occasions when the chauffeur is more economical in terms of real cost).[13]

Here is how it played out: it was Thursday night, I was flying from Melbourne to Perth at the end of a long work week, and there was a torrential downpour which flooded many of the Melbourne city streets and caused traffic backups all around the city. Though I had allowed two hours for this commute that normally takes 40 minutes in peak traffic, it wasn't enough because my taxi driver went the route he was used to taking that he determined would likely get me to the airport on time. But, having driven this trip several times before with a hired chauffeur driver, I knew it happened to be the route that would give the driver the maximum fare. Remember, taxi drivers get paid more the longer the passenger is in the car. Contrast that with a chauffeur who gets paid by the job. For the taxi driver, that trip makes him $100 only when it takes two hours and the longest route. For the chauffeur, the trip is a $100 flat rate, whether it takes one hour or two (and in the past, it has only taken an hour, at most, with the chauffeur, regardless of weather or traffic). I had done my best in advance to explain to my client that my eighteen trips to Australia in a five-year time frame led me to believe it would be in their best interest to hire a driver because, like the weather, Melbourne traffic can be very unpredictable. My client was insistent that this was the new budget allowance, and the taxi was the only option. Against my better judgment, and being too exhausted to try to reason with them, I agreed to their terms. When I finally arrived at the Melbourne airport via taxi, it was twenty-five minutes before my flight was scheduled to depart. The baggage check-in time closed thirty minutes prior to departure, and I could not check my bag.

As I stood at the Qantas counter, I was feeling a mixture of frustration and foolishness. Frustration because now I was bumped from my original flight to one scheduled three hours later, and I still had to fly four hours, adjust to a different time-zone, and rise early the next morning bright-eyed and eager to represent my client and give a wonderful presentation to 100 people! I felt foolish because when it came to travel, I knew better and I went against my better judgment. I needed to have made the decision to pay for the chauffeur even if it was an extra $50 out of my pocket—not making that $50 decision was about to cost me a good night's sleep, a good attitude, sales effectiveness in my presentation, and possibly my health and well-being for the next few days.

In the midst of this, I had two integrity choices: I could either take out my frustration and anger on the gate agents who were doing their jobs *or* accept my circumstances and be kind and gracious to all the people I encountered during my mishap. Fortunately, I chose the latter.

As I stood at the check-in counter holding back the tears that were welling up inside of me, I gently and politely asked if there was any way they could make an exception and get my bag onto the original flight. The Qantas agent was polite but firm in saying no, that wasn't an option—explaining that Qantas has a very strict baggage policy. I humbly accepted the terms, left the counter and made my way to the Qantas Club.

To my surprise, when I arrived at the club, the woman at the desk looked up at me while she was on the phone, signaled for me to come over to verify my Qantas membership then said to the person on the other end of the phone "Yes, Mrs. Dawn Jones is standing in front of me right now." She then finished her conversation and said to me, "Mrs. Jones, your original earlier flight has been delayed. Therefore, the supervisor from the check-in counter called to inform me that because of the delay, if it was all right with you, she was going to switch you back to your original flight, which is boarding right now. Is that all right?" I enthusiastically said, "Yes, of course!" She then informed me that they were holding the flight to allow enough time for me to get to the gate and for them to unload my checked bag from one plane onto the other. I was elated! I was now ready to cry tears of joy!

As the plane departed and I comfortably reclined in my seat, I thought of all the different ways this could have turned out. What if I had been demanding or sarcastic or tried to flaunt my frequent flyer status— how would things have turned out? I was so thankful that I accepted the original terms—even though initially it meant not getting my way. And I was so grateful for the kindness Qantas extended. By the way, the supervisor who told me during the check-in process that she couldn't make any exceptions was a *woman*— the same woman who called the Qantas club to notify me that my original flight was now available and she could switch me back; the same woman who had my luggage unloaded from one plane and loaded onto the other; the same woman who had the flight gate remain open to accommodate this switch. This is a reminder to me that because women are more emotionally attached to their decisions, they are more accommodating when it comes to changing their decisions if they feel or believe it is the right thing to do.

In the infamous neuroscience studies done in collaboration with Baylor University, Cal-Tech's Colin Camerer "...found a surprising effect of gender. When men decide, the area used to process potential reward and calculate numbers is active. The male brains are just "doing the math" and *turn off* after they have made a decision. The female brains are quite different. After women have decided, areas of the brain active in processing potential reward and in regulating worry and error-detection are active. The women are worrying, and thinking about the reward consequences *after* they have decided a course of action."[14] If the gate supervisor had been a man, would he have thought to accommodate me when he saw that my original flight was delayed? Perhaps. The question here is, are you thinking about your customers *after* the sale?

On a side note, the person from the American company responsible for travel budget decisions was also a woman. I believe she did not approve the budget change, in part because my correspondence with her was via email. If a woman can hear or see the genuineness in your request via the phone or face-to-face, she's more inclined to make a change; whereas if she receives an email, the only tone it has is one based on the relationship she has with the sender tied into whatever else is going on in her life at that moment.

An exclamation point from one sender in an email can mean happy, yet from another sender or at a different time it can mean frustration. In the case of the woman in the American company, in my past communications with her, like the Qantas woman, she too has made policy exceptions on a case by case basis—usually by phone, rarely by email, and never after the fact.

Once again I was reminded to be the same person publically, privately, and secretly—especially because character reflects integrity which is *revealed* under pressure. Obviously, this is a lifelong practice. There are days when I regret my response under pressure and I must challenge myself to be the woman that I say I am whether or not someone is looking—whether or not I get my way, which brings this back to you. Who you are and how you react forms your character. Your character comes from what you think about, listen to, watch, read, talk about, and who you hang out with. All of that forms the level of integrity that you bring to any sale and ultimately to your public, private and secret life. Are you willing to commit to being a person of integrity, even if it means not getting your way or not getting the sale? If the answer is yes, you will see this reflected in an increase in sales and a higher quality of relationships and life.

A McMaster University survey of more than 600 board directors showed that women are more likely to consider the rights of others and to take a cooperative approach to decision-making. Male directors, who made up 75% of the survey sample, prefer to make decisions using rules, regulations, and traditional ways of doing business or getting along. Female directors, in contrast, are less constrained by these parameters and are more prepared to rock the boat than their male counterparts.

In addition, women corporate directors are significantly more inclined to make decisions by taking the interests of multiple stakeholders into account in order to arrive at a fair and moral decision. They will also tend to use cooperation, collaboration, and consensus-building more often—and more effectively—in order to make sound decisions.[15]

Just as integrity is fundamental in any sales transaction, so is bringing mastery to your craft. Mastery demonstrates that you are willing to go beyond average or mediocre. It demonstrates that you care about the big picture as well as the details and are in this for the long-run. The way to gain mastery in sales is to **learn, practice,** and **teach**.

Learn your craft: Take the necessary time to study from those who have gone before you. Listen to, watch, read, and participate in teachings that will hone and sharpen your sales skills.

Practice what you learn: Apply the knowledge you gain to your day-to-day work and life.

Teach what you've learned: By helping others learn and grow, you come to a whole new level of mastery within your craft.

The way to incorporate learning, practicing, and teaching into your life is to implement what I like to call the triple T's: **tips, techniques,** and **tools.**

Tips: What I refer to as a tip is an idea, suggestion, or tidbit of knowledge. An example of a tip might be, "begin with the end in mind." This tip is habit number two from the timeless classic *The 7 Habits of Highly Effective People* by Dr. Stephen Covey. You may have heard "begin with the end in mind" somewhere in life. When you're selling to women, what end do you have in mind? What do you want your client to leave with?

Picturing that in your head starts moving you down the path of asking what's in it for her. How is she going to benefit from this? Why does she need this product or this service that you're selling? What is it going to do for the person on the receiving end? Just that one tip of beginning with the end in mind gives you a target to focus on in your sales presentation and prepares you to answer the barrage of questions likely to come from female clients.

Techniques: Techniques are suggestions for implementing the tip. A technique for beginning with the end in mind is to *plan your work and work your plan.* That almost sounds like a tip, doesn't it? Well, it would be if I just left you there.

Techniques teach you how to accomplish the tip. For example, a technique for planning your work and working your plan is to take fifteen minutes every day for planning, first thing in the morning or at the end of your day. I recommend setting a timer in five-minute increments. Start writing your planning ideas, doing a data dump from your head onto paper or to your computer. You can brainstorm a variety of ideas including what your priorities are, in any sale, in terms of what's in it for the other person; where you are in the sales cycle, which clients are ready to make buying decisions, and the details you need to follow-up, just to mention a few.

As you're doing this, you're still looking at that opening tip of beginning with the end in mind; you're just using a technique of taking fifteen minutes and getting those thoughts out of your head and onto paper. The reason I suggest you set your timer for five-minute increments is because sometimes people start working their plan instead of planning their work when they're in the middle of this exercise.

While you're in the midst of your fifteen minutes of planning, you might be thinking, "Oh, I need to send out some rates and references to a prospective client. I need to follow up with a phone call. I need to check my email." Then in the middle of your planning, you find yourself checking your email or voicemail, and you've moved out of *planning* mode and into *work* mode until your timer goes off at that five-minute break and you say, "Oh, wait! I've got to stop, go back to planning my work for fifteen minutes, and *then* I can begin working my plan."

Now here's what's in it for you. If you plan your work and work your plan every single day, it will shave off between an hour to an hour and a half every day of hidden time-wasters. Now that's a huge return on investment.

Tools: I've given you tips and techniques, now here are tools. Tools are tangible. Books, audio learning courses, digital videos—things that you can reference that help you develop and grow. The tool that I learned this technique from was Stephen Covey's *7 Habits of Highly Effective People*.

What you've done here is learned how to take information in the form of a tip, recognize the power of practicing that tip by repeating successful steps that become techniques that form a productive habit—like fifteen minutes of planning every day. Once the productive habit has been formed, continue to practice it while referring back to the tools (books, audios, digital videos, coaching, and training) that helped create this new habit. This repetition will help you to develop mastery so that the newly practiced habits become a natural part of who you are and the old, unproductive habits like fear or procrastination are replaced with new productive habits that bring success.

Bottom line. When you combine tips, techniques, and tools with integrity, your female clients will see that you are prepared and you can be trusted. What you put into your mind determines what comes out of you during the sales process; including the types of questions you ask and answers you give during the sales process. Let's segue into that in our next chapter. Are your questions talking your prospective clients *into* or *out of* doing business with you?

Chapter 4

Ask Great Questions

Why is important to ask great questions? Well, have you ever found yourself in a sales situation where a woman asked you a question, you thought about it, gave her an answer, and then the conversation stopped? Perhaps you thought to yourself, "I gave her a great answer, why isn't she buying?" or maybe you gave her the answer and she did nothing, so you *pushed for the close*. But rather than closing the sale, instead, the conversation closed, leaving you thinking something along the lines of "ugh, I wish I said that differently?" or "What's her problem?" Well, you're not alone. Many salespeople have experienced a time when they wished they could have taken back their answer or added a great question in conjunction with their answer to keep the conversation flowing and been more effective in their communication. Her "problem" was that her questions weren't answered, or the right ones weren't asked. Asking great questions is especially important when selling to women because women tend to ask more questions than men and expect questions to be answered *and* reciprocated during the sales process.

Because asking great questions is such an intricate part of selling to women, it makes sense to become more intentional by asking the best questions upfront, rather than floundering in your questions and falling behind.

While there are numerous types of questions, did you know there are basically three types of questions you can ask for successful selling? What are they? Do you want me to give you a clue or do you want me to give you the answer? I'll tell you what. I'll give you both a clue and the answer...I just asked all three types of questions.

Let's review them starting with the first type of question.

1. "Did you know there are three types of questions you can ask for successful selling?" I knew when I asked you this question you could only give me one of two answers: either no or yes. This type of question, you may know, is commonly called a closed-ended or yes or no question.

If I were to give this type of a question a color, it would be red—like a stop sign. Red signals danger or warning. Red also reminds you to stop and think before you ask these types of questions because you never want to ask a yes or no question in sales unless you know the answer is going to be yes.

The point with yes or no questions is when you're in the sales process—especially when establishing a rapport or clarifying information with a woman—it is best to ask questions that cause her to be agreeable, not argumentative or defensive. "Yes" answers tend to be more agreeable. "No" answers tend to be more argumentative or defensive.

When looking at making phone calls, selling, or having conversations, I compare yes and no questions to the game of baseball. If you ask a question and she says "no," that is strike one. And just like in baseball, three strikes and you are out.

Only ask yes or no questions when you know the answer is going to be "yes." Does this make sense? Did I just give you a yes or no question? You get the picture, don't you?

Are there exceptions? Yes. For example, if you are conducting a survey or gathering factual information about her, such as her likes or dislikes, or you're comparing her current level of satisfaction (or dissatisfaction) with a problem she is having that your product or service can solve for her. I'll introduce a third exception that requires more explanation in detail after we explore all three questions.

2. The second question I asked you was, "What are they?" What are the three types of questions you should ask? This is called an open-ended question. It's open-ended because you have no idea how the person is going to reply unless you ask a question that has only one main answer, such as, "What is your email address?"

The color of this question is yellow—like a flashing caution sign, so use caution when asking these types of questions. Why? The listener may feel pressure to know the *right* answer. Can you remember a time in school when the teacher asked you a question in front of everyone, and you did not have an answer? What about at a business meeting when someone put you on the spot, and you had no idea what they wanted you to say? Stay away from open-ended questions that might cause your listener to feel stumped or foolish trying to figure out what answer you are looking for from them.

Open-ended questions can either put people on the spot and shut down conversations or open up the flow of communication and allow you to retrieve information. Ask open-ended questions with short answers such as, "What is your name?" or "How many years have you been living here?" You naturally use these in daily conversations already. The main thing to remember, especially when you are selling, is to ask open-ended questions only if you believe the person you're asking knows the answer.

Are there exceptions? Yes, if you have already established rapport, the conversation is flowing, and you want to give them time to talk to you about things in more detail. Again, though, be cautious because these types of questions can very easily give you long, detailed answers that you may not have time to hear or that aren't relevant to the conversation. You know the, "Tell me about yourself" types of questions. These answers can run on anywhere from five to twenty minutes, so use caution.

3. Let's move to the third question: "Do you want me to give you a clue or do you want me to give you the answer?" This is an either/or question because you're giving your listener options, like a multiple-choice question. I label these blue questions because blue is

like the ocean. It's vast. It's unending. It's flowing. It's moving.

Either/or questions are the best types of questions to ask when you want to keep the conversation focused and moving, especially when you are engaging in a sales transaction. You may have noticed the colors that I have given these questions are the primary colors. Yes and no questions are red to remind you to stop and think before you ask that question and to remind you to look for an agreeable answer. Open-ended questions are yellow to remind you to use caution when asking so that you don't stump your listener or enter into lengthy answers, but rather ask the questions that give you the information you're looking for. Either/or questions are blue like the ocean, to remind you that when you include multiple choice options, the conversation can be flowing and effortless and can take you and your listener on a charted course with clear focus and direction. I used primary colors because these are the three basic, primary questions.

Remember the fascination you had as a child with your first set of watercolors, blending blue and yellow to make a whole new color, green? Blend your questions in the same way for more colorful communication. Green means go, so ask an either/or question, and tag on an open-ended question. Ask a yes or no question, and tag on an either/or question. Ask a yes or no question then tag on an open-ended question. Put these questions to work for you so you can be consistently confident in your communication on the phone or face-to-face, especially while you are selling.

There are two steps to keep in mind when you are asking a woman these three types of questions. First, listen to her answers, and second, let her know you *heard* her answers. While this advice may seem obvious, I've included it as part of the steps for asking great questions because you'd be surprised how many salespeople skip these steps. Most salespeople either quit listening because they are focused on what questions to ask her next, or, their questions are not prepared and the conversation wanders off course. When I say let her answer, my emphasis is on letting her give you *her* words. As Sherry Prindle likes to say, "A person can argue with *your* words, but it's much harder to argue against themselves."

When Chet sold us our boat, he asked me great questions that he wove into our conversation. He listened to what my husband and I were looking for; then he strategically interjected simple, yet intentional questions such as, "Are you looking for a power boat or a sail boat? Did you have a boat length in mind? Do you want to look at a few boats first? What budget do you want to stay within? When did you want to be living on your boat? This month, next month or do you have a specific date in mind?"

Chet naturally wove the three types of questions into our conversation because he was prepared, intentional, and he listened to the answers. When a woman is telling you her story, she is telling you why she wants to buy something. You see, she still has *something* that she needs and you may be the provider of her solution. Once you have heard her, you can now let her know by validating her and naturally moving great questions into your conversation. Questions that naturally guide her toward your product or service.

This is a good place to ask yes or no questions and to further explore and anticipate "no" being an answer she might give to one of your questions. Because women and men's minds are wired differently, women tend to link more emotional pain to their poor choices than men do. Research shows that this is partially why men tend to take more risks than women. Generally speaking, if a woman makes a decision that causes her, or someone she loves, pain or negative consequences, she is more inclined to remember that incident vividly. For example, think about the types of things women remember when in an argument. Women have the amazing ability to remember a hurtful or painful emotional moment in such great detail that when a woman re-tells her story, like we talked about earlier, it's as if she's reliving a sad scene from an old movie and watching it painfully unfold in slow motion right before your very eyes—you can FEEL it! Contrast that with how a man remembers a painful situation. While he feels the pain, it is usually being processed from an analytical or physical standpoint NOT an emotional one—at least not in front of you. A woman doesn't want to make the same mistake again because she feels more deeply that her mistake is a reflection of her worth as a person; whereas a man is more inclined to risk and try again because the pain of his ego is more involved than his emotions. Women tend to see their mistakes or poor choices as a reflection of their judgment or character; men tend to see their mistakes as reflections of their ability or competency. A woman tends to feel bad if she believes she has exercised poor judgment in a given situation. A man tends to feel foolish if it appears he had poor ability or was incompetent in a given situation.

Let's tie this back into the exception of anticipating "no" as an answer when asking a woman yes or no questions during the sales process. If she has told you about her past decision having a bad outcome, explore that with her—let her tell you her story—and when you listen to what she has to say *and* reflect back to her that you *heard* her, she will be more inclined to listen to you when you tell her that you have a solution. When you are reflecting back to her, you can ask a question such as "I can imagine you wouldn't want to re-live that situation again, would you?" her natural response would be something along the line of "No, I don't want to go through that again." At this point reassure her that she's making a good decision now with you and your company, then keep moving forward.

Beyond the questions you actually want an answer to are the rhetorical kind. The rhetorical kind? Yes, what if you could get a woman to talk herself into wanting to do business with you? I'm not talking about manipulation here. But because women like to explore the facts and expand beyond their original intentions, when selling to them, try some techniques that get them answering their own questions. Backtracking, hypotheticals, and pre-calls can do the trick.

Just like before, I used these three techniques in the previous paragraph. "The rhetorical kind?" was an example of **backtracking** or repeating what the other person said. In this case, when a woman asks a question, rather than going into a long left-brain lecture on facts and specs, try repeating her question back to her in *her* words. She will rethink the question and rephrase it to be more specific to what she really needs to know, or she will answer it for herself. In either case, she gets an answer, and you get a more streamlined conversation. Let's say a woman goes into a hardware store to return a hammer. She says, "It hammers two inches to the left." You repeat, "It hammers two inches to the left?" She replies, "No, I mean the handle slips when I try to hammer, and I end up hitting a spot about two inches to the left." Another example might be that you are selling a learning management system to a large organization, and the decision maker says, "We don't really need training." You respond, "You don't really need training?" and she says, "Well, we do need training, but our employees don't respond well to online training." Notice how easy it was to get clarification just by backtracking and asking a rhetorical question? How much time and irritation have you just saved not launching into a long conversation about why she needs training, when that wasn't the issue at all.

While you always want to backtrack your clients' concerns to signal you have understood, be careful not to overdo repeating her questions. Backtracking is a technique you can use sparingly to get the client to take back or change questions you fear will take you down a rabbit hole.

Hypothetical questions that ask clients to speculate, "What if you could get a woman to talk herself into wanting to do business with you?" was the question I asked to exhibit a hypothetical question. I recommended you use them to overcome the fear of selling. "If" is the main word used to craft a hypothetical, and asking hypothetical questions frees the client to explore how she really feels without the pressure of commitment. Switch to a hypothetical when the client starts saying she doesn't know or doesn't care, "If it did matter to you, which one would you go with?" You can use hypotheticals to explore objections: "If money were no object, which model would you be interested in?" You can hypothetically clarify requests: "If we were more 'responsive,' what would we be doing differently?" Hypothetical exploration is a great way to help women feel understood: "If we were to work together on this, what would you like to see?" Hypothetical questions are also related to the visioning. "How much more efficiently would your team accomplish tasks if..."

Pre-calling is a technique used to confront the negative ruminating women are prone to do when considering buying options. To pre-call means to address potential objections up front, so they don't come up during or after the sales conversation. I was pre-calling when I said, "I'm not talking about manipulation here." Let's say you are offering to do a presentation for the accounting team, and you know their time is precious and that they typically have no patience with high-pressure sales. So when you propose a meeting to the female comptroller, you pre-call like this: "Out of respect for the value of their time, we have prepared a packet for each accountant that contains all the specifications and frequently asked questions about our product as well as diagrams and audit results. We want to give them a chance to look it over and will deliver our program in a Q and A format with no formal sales pitch. You probably need to consult your schedule; so would you like me to call back this afternoon or would tomorrow be better?"

While we are on the subject of questions, also be prepared to field them, lots of them. Remember women research and ask questions. They need all information and details before they will close the deal. Because men oftentimes view this as weak or indecisive, they can be condescending toward women without ever realizing it.[16]

Asking great questions work! But, what makes them work successfully is the level of genuineness and preparedness you bring to the table. I can give advice all day on the best questions to ask and how to position yourself, but people can sense when you are using a technique on them versus when you are sincere and intentional. With women especially, you must be prepared and sincere in order for your intentions to be well received.

When women were exposed to sales messages, they experienced a greater variety and of emotions overall. And only women statistically experience strong emotions related to trust[17]. Because women have positive and negative emotions during the sales process—especially when related to trust—you can minimize the negative emotions by eliminating the "sales pitch" from your phone calls, emails, and face-to-face sales conversations. This allows you to relax and just have a conversation. It lets your female clients know that you're not here to make a quick buck then move on, but instead you're here for the long-run. It says, "I care about getting to know you and the needs of your people, to see if what I have to offer is something you want."

Conversely, have you ever received a phone call from someone trying to sell you something? Though they were a complete stranger, you could hear it in their voice, they came across with an overfriendly, sickly-sweet greeting such as *"Hi, Mr/s. Smith, how are you this evening?"* You knew immediately that this was a "sales call" and that the person on the other end really didn't care how you were that evening! Your brain searched frantically for every possible polite way to hang up the phone all the while the caller continued with their "sales pitch". The reason this type of call is so annoying is because you believe that the "intent" of the caller is to "sell" you something you probably don't need.

Eliminating the sales pitch starts by asking yourself three simple questions *before* making your call. The first question to ask is "what's my intent?"—what's the intent or purpose of the call? The second question is "What questions am I going to ask?" and the third question is "What will be the effect of this phone call?" Intent; questions; effect.

If your intent is to discover what she needs and provide a solution for her, versus *getting the sale,* then your focus becomes dialoguing what's important to her—not telling her what's important to you. By hearing her wishes and talking about them with her, you eliminate the sales pitch. Contrast that with the negative tension that occurs if she's given an ultimatum to buy something you're selling. Once your intent has been established, you can naturally choose questions that will help you both determine if she wants what you have.

The questions you ask and the way you ask them will determine the results you get as well as the effect of your call.

Some tips that will help you sound more natural include mirroring the tone and tempo of her voice. If she answers the phone and sounds as though she has all the time in the world—something like, "ABC company, Judy speaking, how may I direct your call?" Then slow down your tempo and tone to match hers and say who you are and where you're calling from—start the conversation in a more relaxed manner, something like "Hi Judy, this is Dawn Jones from Successful Training Solutions." If she sounds perky and upbeat when she answers the phone saying something like "Hi this is Judy, how can I help you?" This time match or mirror her voice and tempo by speeding up and sounding perky right back to her, but still say the same words "Hi Judy, this is Dawn Jones from Successful Training Solutions!" If Judy sounds a bit rushed and curt, like "ABC company, how may I direct your call?" Then match her speed and tone by saying in a clipped tone and a faster tempo "Hi this is Dawn from Successful Training Solutions." By matching her tempo and tone, the conversation feels more natural to the woman you're calling! Though it might *feel* unnatural to you, you can gradually bring her to your tempo and tone during the conversation, but begin by meeting her where *she is*, then gradually lead her where you want her to go!

An additional tip when it comes to asking great questions addresses how to stop getting the run around when you're following-up with a potential customer. Getting the run-around from someone you're trying to sell something that can happen several different ways. Perhaps you've been trying to reach your contact by phone, and you keep getting voicemail; when you finally do reach her, she tells you she's busy and asks you to please call back. You do call back then she asks you to re-submit your material, letting you know that somehow what you originally sent her has been misplaced or been deleted from her computer files—or she suggests that she never received it. At this point, you may feel frustrated, maybe even a little irritated to say the least!

Two things will help you stop getting the runaround. The first is what you say, including the questions you ask when you finally do reach your contact. The second is your attitude. Remember, your job is to make selling your product or service as easy and painless as possible—that includes giving people the benefit of the doubt even when they give you a reason to feel a little bugged—cut em' some slack. The people you're attempting to follow-up with have other responsibilities and oftentimes what you're selling becomes a low priority for them. It's not that what you have to offer isn't important or of value; it's that they simply have other priorities right now. What you say and how you say it will cause you to become either a higher or lower priority.

So keep a good attitude and let's look at some good questions you can ask to become a higher priority. Start by being specific. What is the purpose or intent of the call? What do you want to find out? Then ask one, two or three specific things. You can do this using voicemail or email. The worst voicemail is one where the caller leaves little or no valuable information such as "Hi, this is Mike returning your call, get back to me when you can." Now you notice that Mike said who he was, but he didn't say what his last name is or where he's calling from or even the reason for his call and, most importantly, he didn't leave a phone number. So be specific when you leave a voicemail or when you're speaking with the person. Do you want to find something out or give some information?

If you want to talk with someone, and you get them on to the phone, what do you want to accomplish with them? Again, be specific. Specific questions get specific answers; vague questions get vague answers—or worse, they get no answers, especially with voicemail. Which leads to being *put-off* instead of called back.

Let's go back and look at our call with Mike, and try that again. With a good attitude, Mike could say something like, "Hi Susie, this is Mike calling from Your Favorite Company. I just wanted to check back with you to make sure you received the materials I sent you. I'll try to call you a little later today or sometime tomorrow unless I hear from you sooner. Again, my number is (206) 555-1212 thanks, Susie I'll talk with you then. Bye."

Notice how much more personable this voicemail was? Prior to picking up the phone, Mike remembered to check his attitude to make sure it was good; then when he called Susie, he stated her name both at the beginning of the voicemail as well as at the end. He said who he was and where he was calling from along with the purpose of his call. He clearly left his phone number and then stated that he would call her back, *and* he also gave Susie the option of calling him first. The next thing for Mike to do is deliver what he promised. To call her back and ask her the same questions perhaps changing them slightly by starting out with "just wanted to make sure you had a chance to review the materials I sent you."

When being intentional with your questions, limit yourself to 1 to 3 questions and state those questions upfront so that she knows you're looking for specific answers. Let's say that Mike was selling real estate and he had a property that would perfectly fit Susie's needs. He might say something like, "Hi Susie, Mike here from your Favorite Real Estate Company. I have three quick questions for you because I believe I've found the perfect property that fits almost all the criteria you said you were looking for. First, do you still want a property with a beach-front view and second, is it okay if it is a few miles beyond the area you originally targeted and third, is it all right that it's several thousand dollars *under* the budget you wanted to spend? All right Susie, call me back as soon as you can so we can get you out here to see it! As you know, my number is (206)...Looking forward to connecting soon. Bye."

Once again, this voicemail is even more specific than the one before. Even though the property is a few miles beyond the location where she's looking, and she might say no, he positioned that question between two yes questions—beach view and lower price. This same standard applies regardless of what you are selling—the principles are the same—to stop getting the run-around, ask intentional and specific questions.

If you're a businessperson or a speaker looking to schedule a meeting or book some training, try something similar to this:

Hi Linda, David here, just getting back to you regarding the info I emailed you in response to your company training needs. I have a couple of quick questions. First, what are the most important things you want to accomplish during your training?...Would that be for participants to interact and implement what they're learning during class time and demonstrate their confidence by applying what they've learned that day; or staying within your budget; or both? Secondly, do you prefer a 3-5 hour highly interactive training session with a lot of "hands on" participation? Or do you want a shorter session—more of a keynote style where we cover the main points with examples and move onto the next topic? I'll check back with you to see what works best—or feel free to send me an email at david@yourfavoiritetraining.com or call me at 800-555-1212.

Remember to say your phone number and email address s-l-o-w-l-y and clearly! Spell it out if needed. Don't mumble or rush. If there are letters such as "S" or "F" remember to say, "S" like Sam or "F" like Frank. And a bonus tip with regards to your own personal email, do your best to get a simple email address—or website— keep it short and memorable, not long and artsy. Make it easy for people to remember you *and* find you—so they can find you and buy what you are selling!

The final technique I want to address when it comes to asking great questions is getting called back not put off. This is a vital step when it comes to successfully selling to women. Much like how to stop getting the runaround, remember to be specific with your questions and keep a good attitude. Some reasons women put you off include: not knowing enough about you and your services, or they *don't* want your services yet and don't know how to tell you. Or they're not the person who makes that decision. In my over 20-years of experience in working with business people, executives, and entrepreneurs, I have found that the main reason people put you off is because they're busy with their own priorities and just haven't had time to get back with you.

When being put-off, what happens is you call the person and either go directly to voicemail or worse, the assistant asks you "Who is calling?" Then puts you on hold. Then the assistant returns, and says, "I'm sorry, she's not available, can I put you through to her voicemail?" So what do you do? If this isn't the first time being put off, most people go to voicemail and feel discouraged—then that discouragement comes through in their tone—and the voicemail sounds somewhat despondent "Hi Jennifer, this is John from Confident Training Solutions, um, I'll just try back again later."

Now how confident did John from Confident Training Solutions really sound to you? If you were the person thinking about booking John to provide your training, would this voicemail prompt you to call him back? Me neither! So when you're the salesperson preparing to call someone back, instead of being discouraged when you're being transferred to your prospective client's voicemail, instead you can be prepared with great questions and a great attitude—I mean think about it—you have a captive audience that will listen to you for up to three minutes via voicemail, so make it count! Remember to remind yourself why she needs what you're selling, be prepared with your two to three questions, smile when you speak, even make reference to something humorous or relevant to her from your previous conversation. All of these intentional thoughts and actions will help keep you focused on why she wants what you have rather than focused on why she's not calling you back. Bottom line here is to give her *reasons* to call you back rather than *excuses to* put you off!

Here are some things to keep in mind prior to articulating your voice message. Perhaps you've spoken with your prospective client, and you know that she's responsible for the buying decision. When you attempt to follow up with her, she never seems to be available. Let's review a few reasons for the runaround:

- She's not clear on what you're offering her
- She doesn't know what you want from her
- She doesn't have an answer for your yet
- She's not convinced that she wants what you're selling
- She forgot about you
- She's not good at making decisions without help
- Or worse, she's not the person you need to be speaking with!

There are three simple steps you can take to get called back rather than put off.

First, **be persistent and consistent. Persistent**: Follow-up with at least three to five calls and/or emails to her before you move on. **Consistent:** Repeat the same reasons for contacting her when you leave your voicemail or send your email. (Remember the Big-Mac commercial? "Two all-beef patties..." you know the rest) people need to be reminded of what you're offering so that they can remember who you are and exactly what it is you're calling about. Even though you may have left the same voicemail with 15 different people today, each person you're leaving it with is hearing it for the first time! If you change your voicemail—you dilute your message and can cause confusion—which leads to being put off rather than called back. Be consistent and persistent!

The next step is to **LISTEN**! Listen to what she says about how she's going to make her buying decision. Perhaps she says "We'll be having a meeting next Thursday to finalize our purchasing decision." Repeat back to her something like: "Okay, you'll be deciding next Thursday who you're going to schedule, great; would it be better if I checked back with you Friday or Monday to go over those details?" Regardless of whether she tells you to call back Friday, Monday or that they'll call you back; in order to separate yourself from the average person trying to get her business—here's where you go above and beyond her expectations. On the Wednesday night before their meeting, send her an email thanking her and her team for considering you and your services. Include bullet points reminding them what they'll receive if they choose you. Also, remind them that you'll check back with them in a few days unless you hear from them sooner. When you LISTEN to what they want, you can respond by giving them what they need— when THEY need it.

Finally, **be easy to work with**. This is the easiest step to implement *if* you implement it! Remember to have a servant attitude. This is where you go out of your way to make it easy for her to choose to do business with you. Do this by being easy to work with—if she forgets to call you back or doesn't give you the answer when promised—or she just doesn't respond to your emails or voicemails, don't sweat it! Just give her a chance to save face and to start over. Bear in mind that when people don't return your calls or haven't fulfilled a promise to you, they might feel bad, as though they've let you down, therefore, they might avoid calling you back. Again, separate yourself from the average salesperson by extending them grace—again, *cut em' some slack!* Let her know that you understand that she has a full schedule and thank her again for taking the time to consider your product/services. Then, gently remind her as to why she needs what you have and how you can help her. You get more bees with honey than you do with vinegar. These three simple steps will help you to get called back and not put off!

Now, what if you'd done everything you can to reach her and she keeps giving you the run-around? Here's a bonus, sample voicemail that you can also use as an email to follow-up with someone who's hard to pin down.

I call this the *final follow-up call or email.* Remember to smile and keep your chin up:

"Hi _____ (say the person's name). I just wanted to follow up with you one last time. This is (say your name). I'm sure you've got a lot of things going on right now, and I don't want to be "one more thing" for you put on your list of To-Dos. Since we haven't spoken recently, I'm guessing that there isn't a place for my services that fits your needs at this time. (I understand you have a lot to consider when working with new vendors and again, I appreciate your time and consideration). What I'd like to do is to check back with you in 6-months or so

to see where my services might best serve you and your team. In the meantime, I'll keep you posted as to what's going on by sending you periodic e-mail newsletters. Feel free to contact me if I can be of service to you between now and then. Thank you for your consideration and encouragement and for all you do. Talk with you later (say her name)."

Personalize that presentation to fit you and your prospective client. Remember to include specifically what you're services include, and do check back with her in the time frame you promised. This is another way to increase your credibility while building a relationship with a future client.

Bottom line. Remember, *yes* and *no* questions are red to remind you to stop and think before you ask those questions and to remind you to look for an agreeable answer. *Open-ended questions* are yellow, to remind you to use caution when asking so that you don't stump your listener or enter into lengthy answers, but rather ask the questions that give you the information you're looking for. *Either/or* questions are blue like the ocean to remind you that when you include multiple choice options, you should blend your questions to keep the conversation flowing.

Periodically repeat her questions back to her using backtracking and rhetorical questions only if you are receiving a contradictory message such as "we don't need training." Incorporate hypothetical questions when she says something like "I don't know what I want." By responding with "Let's pretend you could choose anything, what would that look like?" And use pre-calling questions if you think she might have an objection such as the example when the realtor said the property was a few miles beyond the buyer's desired target location. Listen to her answers and adjust your questions according to her priorities, not your sales presentation script.

Remember the three simple steps of being consistent and persistent, listening to what she needs and being easy to work with. Do these in conjunction with using the suggested techniques including the final follow-up call or email to help you determine whether it's time to set an appointment date, time to wait or time to move on. And lastly, re-read this chapter weekly—especially before a sales presentation—you can even leave yourself a voicemail of you reading the questions, then go back and listen to it so that you can hear what your clients hear when you call them—do these things to quickly become more natural when asking great questions.

Chapter 5

Integrate All Four Communication Styles

Read this section to get in touch with communication modalities, does that sound good? You see, every person you meet has a preferred method of communicating, and I incorporated all four into these two sentences.

The four communication styles are: verbal, visual, tactile (hands-on), and written word. Let's take them one at a time.

Verbal. According to the University of Missouri, 44 percent of the people you communicate with need to hear instructions. Here's the challenge. If that's the only method of communication or sales that you're using, they need to hear what you're saying six to ten times. That's a lot of repetition. If you listen to something repeatedly, you're going to take in the information much faster and find that it's coming out of your mouth much quicker because you're listening to something until it becomes your thoughts. That is the beauty of audio programs, for example.

Here's the drawback. If you've ever given instructions to someone, and you're thinking to yourself, "I have told that person four times how to do this," congratulations! You're halfway there. Yes, they need to hear it six to ten times in order for them to *get it*. Remember, when you are selling to somebody, they're going to ask you questions, and they're going to listen when it is important to *them*. Even if you've already told them six to ten times, they don't hear it until it's important to them. That's why when you're listening to a commercial on the radio, they'll oftentimes repeat the phone number, website address, or price of the item two or three times during the commercial.

Now, I'm going to prove it to you. Regardless of what you're eating habits are, regardless if you're a vegetarian, or if you're a carnivore, you can tell me the answer to this question, unless you've been living in a cave for the last twenty years.

Here's the question. What is on a Big Mac? I can hear you right now, *two all-beef patties, special sauce, lettuce, cheese, pickles, onions, on a sesame-seed bun.* Case in point.

That commercial and that promotion haven't been around for years, yet you can still remember what is on a Big Mac just because of the power of repetition. Anthony Robbins says, "Repetition is the mother of skill." If you want to get good at something, learn how to do it. Listen to it repeatedly. If you want to master something, teach other people how to do it. That's the verbal technique.

Visual. This is the fastest way to teach someone a concept. YouTube and internet videos are so popular because they show you how to do something just like that—in the blink of an eye or the watching of a video clip.

Now back in the "olden days," like twenty years ago, if you had a problem with your computer, you would usually go to the source, and there would be a help menu with written words in technical jargon; it was almost like learning a new language.

At that time, entrepreneurs, creative people, and sales and marketing people thought to themselves, "How can we take these complex ideas and get people to understand them? Let's make a video." That's when those little video clips were born. Visual is the fastest way to teach somebody a concept.

If you show *and* tell someone how to do something, you will get your point across very quickly, especially when you're in sales. I do want to caution you here that if they don't get the experience of doing it themselves, you may just be creating what I like to call the *armchair quarterback*.

The armchair quarterback is that fan who's watching an American football game, watching the quarterback, and watching the plays, then watching the players on the field. The armchair quarterback can call the plays before they happen. They can even call the right terms, and they can call the interception. They've got their favorite team. They know the rules. They're passionate about it. They paint their faces and wear team colors. You get the idea.

The problem is that if you were to throw that passionate fan into the middle of a game where the professionals were actually playing—and expect that fan to be a player—the audience would think they were the halftime show because that armchair quarterback hasn't run a play in years, if ever. You don't want to be guilty of being an armchair quarterback; you know the one who says, "I've heard this before. I know this. I've seen this done before. I could probably stand up and do that very same thing that she's talking about right now."

Unless you move to that third stage, you will always be the armchair quarterback thinking, "I could have been a contender. I could have done this." So let's *do* it; let's move to that third stage, that tactile, hands-on stage.

Tactile. This is the best way for people to remember something. When you're in the middle of a sales process, yes, you tell them your intentions. Yes, you ask them questions. Yes, you show them the benefits. Yes, you identify what's in it for them. And then you put that person in the scene; have them picture that end in mind, what it is going to do for them. Have them see the big picture vision of what your service or product is going to do for them. It will bring them freedom, provide financial independence, and give them time to spend with their family, or plan their retirement. Give them that visual end in mind. Then let them actually try or do exactly what you're talking to them about. Again, the best way for somebody to grasp your concepts is just to let them do it—let them experience it.

Written Word. According to the Literacy Company, the written word is one of the most challenging learning styles because most adults are reading at a grade school level. Most adults are still reading one word at a time. Think about how many emails you get in a day, how many letters of correspondence you receive, how many journals and periodicals you read, how many books you read (there are some pretty staggering statistics indicating that a lot of people don't read books after they get out of high school or college).

Think about what the last book you read was, or did you listen to something, or did you watch something or did you participate in something? But the written word is really powerful. Not only does it improve your memory, and your intelligence, it also improves your learning levels. Yet a lot of people struggle with reading. The average reading speed in America is about 300 to 350 words per minute. This is grade school or primary school level.

You might be thinking, "No, it can't be." But if you do the research, you will see. In fact, the Literacy Company has gone so far as to predict, with the State of Arizona, how many adult offender prison beds to have for future offenders by testing fourth-grade reading level. There are a lot of people who hide the fact that they struggle with reading.

Let's say a student begins the fourth grade struggling with reading. They're going to hide it because they don't want to be uncool or feel foolish. In fact, one of many people's biggest fears is the fear of being judged by other people, and so these kids drop off of the radar. They can't keep up in fourth grade. They can't keep up in fifth grade. They start making poor choices. They hang out with other people who can't keep up, and you can see where this goes.

This hits home for me personally. I struggled with reading all of my life, and it wasn't until I was 40 that I found a tool that helped me stop reading like a child and start reading like a grown up. This tool took me from 236 words a minute at 50 percent comprehension up to over 1,000 words a minute at 85 percent comprehension. I had struggled with undiagnosed dyslexia and undiagnosed ADD. I just thought I was the problem. When I found out it wasn't me, reading opened up a whole new world to me and I am very grateful, as it has changed my life and the lives of countless others who have overcome this challenge.

Let's tie the verbal, visual, tactile and the written word learning styles into the selling process. Be prepared with your talk. Be prepared with your visuals. Be prepared with engaging your customer in that sales process and have things in writing. A bonus technique on this: create an outline of what you want your customer to leave with. You don't want to overwhelm them with writing or data; provide them with an outline and let them write down what's important to them. If you say something during the sales process that is important to them, and they're so engaged in the conversation that they don't write it down, you catch that moment and say, "Oh, this is important; you may want to write this one down." I want you to remember this as you're thinking about the sales process.

Keep the different communication modalities in mind when selling to women because men and women purchase differently and want different interactions verbally, visually, tactically, and when reading the written word. Regardless of what modality you are using, men are usually more transactional. In a sense, they want to close the deal and be done with it. Women are more relational (unless they are rushed and just popping in the store to grab something like a forgotten grocery item). Moreover, most women want to experience a connection with you and your environment in their buying process. They want to like you and come back to your place of business. Women tend to place a higher value on establishing a relationship and a high-quality buying experience than they do on being loyal to a product or its price.

With these modalities in mind, men and women purchase differently. Men are generally more focused on getting the best price for the highest quality, in the least amount of acquisition time; whereas women are more interested in learning about the quality of a product or service and taking the time to compare similar items in order to get the right product or service that meets their needs.

There are many communication differences you should expect when selling to a woman. Women tend to be more engaged verbally by asking questions, especially assurance type questions. They are less concerned with reading about the mechanics of a product or service and are more concerned with making the right decision. For example, if purchasing a car, a woman will care less about engine size and more about its safety rating. She is less concerned about how quickly it goes from zero to sixty and cares more about the look and feel of the interior.

When talking with a salesperson, men tend to want facts and figures. Women want to know the *why* behind the *what*. Give it to them. Keep in mind that if a man doesn't know the answer to a question about the product or service, he is less inclined to ask for help (aka, not asking for directions), whereas women tend to be more open if they don't know something and will ask for more information so they can make a better choice.

Prior to finalizing the sale, women tend to ask detailed questions that are important to them. Some salespeople may think the women are asking too many questions or trying to be difficult. This is where women are very different than men. Before a woman completes the sales transaction, she wants to make sure all of her questions are answered so that she's confident she is making the best choice—with no regrets. More dialogue and more answers mean an increased likelihood of the sale being closed. Men, on the other hand, can enter into a battle of wits when questions are being asked. There is a posturing that occurs between men when engaging in questions that create a competitive tension. Whoever has the best answers wins, per se. Because of this competitive tension, men often view too much questioning as weak or indecisive. As stated earlier, those types of salespeople can come across as being condescending toward women without ever realizing it.

Friends of mine recently went shopping for a new car. They shopped at several car dealerships and had very different experiences. First, they had to eliminate the dealerships with the salespeople who just wanted to *make the sale*. They narrowed it down to two dealerships. During both shopping experiences, the wife stated she really wanted a specific car model with a sunroof and she preferred leather interior rather than cloth. She also had a budget she wanted to stay within. Because the car was for her, she was very specific about her preferences; and, her husband lets both car salesmen know that she was very particular and whoever could find what she was looking for, would get the sale.

At the first dealership they visited, the salesperson seemed to get irritated with all of the particulars she was looking for—especially considering the budget she was bringing to the table. As a result, he tried to sell her the newer car models that had fewer features, and the answers he provided were short and dismissive. Even her husband began rolling his eyes at one point. At the second dealership, the salesperson confirmed and agreed with her concerns, and he answered all of her questions in a thorough, in-depth manner. He took his time with her. This salesman's approach, and the interest he took in answering her questions, even caused her husband to value the questions she asked and the answers the salesman gave. Can you guess where they ended up purchasing their car? And, by the way, the price for the car she chose at the second dealership was a few thousand dollars over her stated budget.

When salespeople understand how to bring in the different communication modalities, they also understand how these differences influence women to buy. What's important to women is how they buy and who they buy from. They will buy from a person and a business where they feel a sense of connectedness. They will buy from a business with a great reputation, where they receive an outstanding customer experience throughout the sales process.

There are also differences in how men and women shop. When shopping, men like to purchase something specific. They will go into a store, buy what they need and leave. A man tends to shop as though he's on a focused hunting excursion. Before he even set's foot in a store he has decided what he'll be capturing and bringing home—and more than likely he'll be in and out of the store within 20 minutes. If a man needs a new toolbox, he'll decide on the make and model, pick the store, drive directly there, and head straight to the tools section. He'll then pick up his toolbox, purchase it, and leave. The only way he'll buy something different is if it's a toolbox in the same section and is a higher quality product at a better price. Other than that, once the conquest has taken place, he may see something else—like food or a snack while standing in the check-out line—*after* he's made his primary acquisition.

A woman, on the other hand, shops to explore. Even if she knows she only needs a new jacket, she'll walk into the store with more of a browsing mentality—keeping her eyes open for other items that could compliment her wardrobe. In addition to clothing, she'll even shop for other merchandise, and if she likes what she sees she'll leave with a new jacket, a pair of slacks and a matching handbag.

Where men and women are shopping is different too. For men, retail ambiance is the least of their concerns. Whether a retail store or the internet, the decision is made based on how soon he needs to purchase an item and how quickly he can find it. Take for example that hardware store—most men don't care about the ambiance of the store as long as they can find what they need, get the highest quality for the best price, and then get out. On the other hand, women like to go on a shopping experience. They like to explore and get what they need as well as looking to see what they might need. Once in a buying situation, many women find shopping to be a therapeutic experience—hence the term *retail therapy.*

More and more women are taking their shopping and purchasing experiences to the internet. With easy product return and exchange processes available through many online businesses, it is not uncommon for a woman to buy two or three of the same item in different sizes and colors and just return the ones that aren't a fit for her through her local mail courier. Women are also browsing the internet first *then* going to the store to *try it on for size.* If you are selling something in a retail setting, remember that women like to have that hands-on experience. They want to touch and feel the merchandise. They like to have several choices, but don't want to be overwhelmed—remember, a buyer who has too many choices can easily become a confused non-buyer. Women also pay attention to the ambiance of your store. Whether you work in an upscale store or a bargain basement store, make sure your theme ties into your retail environment.

If your store is more bargain-focused, your shopper is usually looking to save money or get a good deal. She is more likely to roll-up her sleeves and go on a hunting expedition, willing to brave the wilds of other predators (aka other shoppers) who might get to the bargaining table before she does. It is okay for this type of store to have high white ceilings and bright fluorescent lighting. For example, if this is a discount clothing store, it is expected that the racks will be tightly crammed with a hodgepodge selection of clothes and that there will be little room to maneuver her shopping cart as she forages the dense rack of clearance items.

Contrast that with an upscale store where a woman is focusing more on quality and atmosphere, and, is willing to pay a higher price for her selections. If you have an upscale store, you want her to feel relaxed, calm, unique, and special. Create that ambiance with rich, neutral tones and colors; allow space for her to move freely within your store; spotlight key products with warm lighting; the flooring should also be warm and welcoming. You can even infuse subtle fragrance into your store which can influence her buying decision towards purchasing from you. The more intentional you are about creating a *female-friendly* store that targets your buyer, the better chance of catching and keeping loyal female customers.

Bottom line. Bring the four communication modalities of visual, verbal, tactile and the written word, to the sale for yourself and also for your customer. Tie that in with a high level of integrity and remember to ask great questions.

Chapter 6

Sell to the Different Personality Types

Let's move on to selling to the different personality types. Contrary to the popular belief that you must be kind and gentle when selling to women, the complete opposite may be true when it comes to personality styles. Have you ever found yourself in a situation where you started a sales presentation with a woman by asking her about her feelings about something? Perhaps it was her feelings about how she was doing today? Or how her family was doing? Or some other type of "small-talk" meant to build rapport by letting her know that you cared—only to be shut down by her releasing an exacerbated sigh, filled with impatience followed by a wide-eyed stern look almost demanding you to *get on with it!* This is where personality comes into play.

In a report published for FONA (Flavors of North America) International, Kit Barmann explores the *Purchasing Power of Women,* citing leading experts on marketing to women. Marti Barletta, who is called the high priestess of marketing to women by the Huffington Post, says "One of the big mistakes companies make is assuming women are all about the warm and fuzzy, and they're not. They want all the same things men do and then some." Anna Shaw from Smart Design, an innovation company with a lab that focuses on female consumers, told *Inc.* magazine that companies flounder when they interpret women as "smaller, softer humans," saying, "Companies need to understand who she is, what are her emotions, what are her values."[18]

I can attest to this research first-hand. As an international speaker, I have the privilege of traveling to different parts of the world and meeting and speaking to people of different cultures and personalities. Though beliefs and values vary within societies, one of the secrets I discovered was that regardless of where I was in the world, there always seemed to be four primary personality styles that surfaced among people. I became so fascinated with this realization, that I began to study the different types and decided to write and record my findings into an audio and e-book that could help other people understand the challenges they may face when interacting with differing personalities— what made this book unique was that I wrote it from an international perspective. At the time, I had no idea how well it would be received by the global community.

On one of my trips to Australia, I got a call from my publisher who said, "Hey, Dawn! I need you to go online to the iTunes website."

I said, "Okay."

He continued, "Now I want you to go to the business audio books section, top 100."

"Okay, I'm there. Now what?"

"Go ahead and do a search for *Top 7 Personality Challenges.*"

"Okay."

"What do you see?"

"Oh, my gosh!" I said. "I'm number 39. My book is number 39. This is so exciting."

I remember hearing, "Ha ha! That's right. Dawn, you're in there. You're in the top 100. Isn't that great? Congratulations! You're an author."

It was very overwhelming. It was very rewarding, and I was very humbled by the whole thing and very appreciative.

After that, it got to be a little bit fun because I started to follow it. I shared it with some people as I was on my speaking tour, and then I watched it go from the 30s to the 20s, into the 10s. I remember it hovering in the top 10 with giants whom I have looked up to for years; I mean Zig Ziglar, Brian Tracy, John Maxwell, even Anthony Robbins. I watched it crawl from 10 to 9 to 5, and there it was. It hit number 1. Apparently it stayed there for 11 weeks, first in Australia, then in America, and then hovered at the top in five European countries.

Now the cool thing to me, just from a human perspective, was thinking, "Wow, this is so possible. Anybody can do something if you give a different, but relevant, perspective on a familiar topic." The second thing it taught me was there was more to dealing with, speaking to, and selling to the different personality styles than just a North American perspective. Because when I put my book together, I had factored in many different cultures including the Australian, New Zealand, African, British culture, North American, and Asian cultures—people and places I've had the privilege of training.

With that in mind, I want you to think about the different personality styles you encounter in your life because I'm going to be teaching some of the concepts from the *Top 7 Personality Challenges*. Now I'm not going to give you all of those challenges, but what I want to give you is an overview of the four primary personality styles. Then I want you to be watching for how to sell successfully to these different styles and, finally, I'll give you some examples on how to do just that.

As you may know, personality styles and quizzes and information about personalities have been around for years. In fact, Greek philosophers back around 450 B.C. came up with the different personality styles and how to be agreeable with each style and how to create win-win situations for each type.

Taking it through the years, you've got things such as Myers-Briggs and DiSC training; you have the animals and even the colors personality quizzes. There are so many variations of personality styles. Really, it comes down to four primary styles.

Yes, they get more complex, but let's begin with the basics. You've got the direct driver type of person. You have the thinker/analyzer person. You have the social extrovert or the innovative type of person. Then you have that relational person.

I'm going to take one at a time and do a quick overview since you are probably familiar with styles. If you're not, this is enough to get you started. What I want you to watch for here is what your style is, and what your favorite styles to sell to are. Then, while you're thinking about that, I want you to think about which styles irritate you and which styles you have a hard time selling to. All right, so keep those things in mind.

Direct, driver type people tend to be fast-paced, bottom-line, get-to-the-point. These are your natural leaders. They are effective decision makers.

The thinker-analyzer personalities tend to be more detailed, meticulous, and accurate. They like things in order. I like to say they were born with a drop-down menu in their head. They have processes, and they love to have a place for everything.

The socializer or the social extroverts are creative and innovative people who tend to be fun loving, energetic, expressive, spontaneous, and the life of the party.

Then that relational person tends to be pretty pleasant, friendly, dependable, and calm. They often take on the role of the peacemaker.

Next, let's give each style a motto and also take a look at some of the challenges that each personality faces.

The motto of the direct person or driver is, "Get it done! Get it done! Get it done!" They don't want excuses. They don't want long explanations. They don't want formulas. They just want you to get it done. Now, they can be challenged with coming from too broad a perspective, from a bird's eye view. One of the challenges that they don't even see about themselves is they sometimes come across as bossy or overbearing. They might see it and not care or appear to not care. Realize when you're selling to the direct style, sometimes they will come across as wanting to take the lead or be bossy or get you to *get to the point.*

Let's move now to the thinker-analyzer. The thinker-analyzer tends to want it to be right. Their motto is, "Do it right! If you're going to do it, do it right." One of the challenges you might face with them is analysis paralysis. They'll go over the details. They can be picky and sometimes demanding. They'll be asking for more than might realistically be possible in the sale, so keep that in mind.

With the socially extroverted, innovative type of person, their motto is, "Get appreciated!" They love to be recognized. In fact, you'll find that you may need to give a lot of appreciation, whether it be in their decision-making or in an *"aha"* that they experienced. You may need to be a little bit more motivated, and a little bit more ramped up when you're speaking with this particular personality type.

Now the relational person's motto is, "Can't we all get along?" They can be challenged if they're making a decision that appears to be selfish or doesn't consider other people. They will often freeze up and become indecisive or uncommunicative.

This was a quick overview of the four primary personality types. For a more detailed description of these styles, you can download a FREE copy of that portion in the *Top 7 Personality Challenges* at www.dawnjones.net and receive the section that goes into the challenges you face with each one. The main thing here is to keep those differences in mind when you're selling to the different styles.

Please realize there are times you're going to be speaking with some people who are direct and also social extroverts, so there are people who want to get things done and have a lot of fun. Also, realize there are going to be times that you're speaking with thinker types who also happen to be relational. You might not be able to read them because they process so much internally. And they're really nice and polite even if things in the sales process aren't adding up for them. While we are all combinations of the four styles, usually you have one or two dominant personality traits.

What I want you to be thinking about as you're reading this is where do you go when under pressure? Do you tend to be the more bottom line, "Let's get it done" type? Do you tend to be the, "Okay, let's analyze. Let's discuss some facts. Let's move to the process, and let's explain this process again" type? Do you tend to be the socializer, the creative-innovative person and have fun and think, "If I just make this more fun, then this person will make the decision and purchase now?" Do you tend to be that relational person that says, "Oh, gosh! Can we all get along? I'd really like you to do this, but at the same time, I don't want to offend you, so if you don't want to do this right now, I'll just come back later." What tends to be your style in that selling situation?

Now I want you to think about which styles tend to be challenging for you. Are you challenged when you're faced with somebody who's asking you for the facts, asking you to get to the bottom line, and leading the conversation almost in an intimidating and intense manner? Or do you thrive in that type of environment? That would, of course, be a more direct environment.

Okay, now for you directors out there, you might be thinking, "Dawn, I got it. Move to the next one." So let's do just that and go to the thinker-analyzer.

When you're working with thinker-analyzers and they're very methodical and asking lots of questions are you thinking, "Yes, this makes sense. I can walk them through the process. This is logical. This is easy. Why can't everyone be this linear?"

Or do you find yourself getting irritated with that style, thinking, "Look, I've already gone over this. I've already told you. What do you mean you want me to bring you a spreadsheet and walk you through the steps, *again*?" What style becomes more dominant in you when you are with that thinker-analyzer?

Let's go on to the social extrovert. Do you find yourself getting really, really jazzed when working with people who are high energy, who can jump from one part of a conversation to another? Do you find yourself affirming the person by saying things such as, "You're amazing; you did a great job?" Or do you find yourself getting scattered with that person, feeling overwhelmed and thinking, "Why do I have to give you so many kudos or so many strokes or tell you how great you are? You're bugging me. You're driving me crazy."

Then there is the relational person. Do you feel comfortable with them, finding it very easy to connect with them? It is very low key, low pressure. Or do you find yourself going, "Come on already, and make a decision? I've given you enough time for this. What do you mean you have to go ask somebody else? How much time do you need on this?" See where you fit when selling to those different styles because that is where personality clashes occur.

Now I'm going to move you into four techniques you can use for successfully selling to those different personalities, regardless of whether they are women or men. Here are the questions to ask yourself when selling to each of the styles, and some specific techniques to accomplish those results.

1. How do you capture the attention of that particular style?
2. What motivates that style to purchase?
3. What irritates that style?
4. What's the best technique for making the sale?

As you go through this, if you are familiar with selling to different personality styles, this will be a great addition to your understanding. On the other hand, if this is something new to you and you're just starting to learn the personality styles, it will give you great insight. Either way, this will provide some answers for when you're faced with a challenging personality, and you find yourself thinking, "How do I sell to this personality style and still be *real* in the process?"

Well, let me give you some of the characteristics, motivators, and techniques so you'll be able to start thinking of clients, thinking of coworkers, thinking of family members, even thinking of yourself with the realization, "Oh, yeah, that is me. Yeah, that is this client."

As I give the characteristic that describes somebody you know in life, I want you to write down their name and their style, so every time I talk about that style, you can picture that person. That's going to make this a little bit more real for you when you implement these techniques.

Let's go to the first one. What captures the attention of that direct, driver-type, bottom-line person? There are two things: they want results and they want to save time and money. I know that's really three things, but to direct people time is money.

Ask yourself, "What does this person want from this? Do they want to feel healthier? Do they want to feel more motivated? Do they want to lose weight? Do they want to feel more successful? What is most important to this person? What results are they going to accomplish and what is the fastest way possible I can get them to those results?" Now let's look at the second component of what motivates them to purchase.

Direct, driver-type personalities like things to move quickly and just want some key facts. It goes like this, "Tell me what it's going to do for me. Tell me how we're going to accomplish that. Okay, now let's just do it. Let's make a decision and move on." They love action. They like to be involved in the big picture part of the process. They like to know you've done your homework, but they don't want to hear it. They are more interested in what it's going to give them in a short period of time.

Now here's the third component, things that can irritate the direct-type people. Here are some of the challenges in working with direct-type people. First of all, getting time with them; that's a big deal. Trying to pin down a director is like trying to capture the wind because when you finally do get them on the phone, or at their office, or by email, they're saying to themselves, "I don't have time right now." I'll give you some techniques for dealing with that in just a moment. The second challenge is honing into what's in it for them and what's important to them because they don't care about you or any stories you have to tell. They are the true epitome of WIIFM, *what's in it for me*, that radio station people listen to in their head 24 hours a day, 7 days a week, 365 days a year. They're asking the whole time, "What's in it for me?"

Because one of the challenges is getting a direct person to listen, make sure you're constantly tuning into what's in it for *them*. There are two times that direct people listen: When it's important to them and when they are speaking. I know that sounds a little bit funny, can they listen when they're speaking? Here is a nugget for you: if it's important to them, they are speaking about it. This is where it's critical for you as the salesperson to listen; listen to what's in it for them. They are telling you, "Here is how you can sell me. If you give me these things, I will make a decision and purchase. If you can't, I'm going to move on."

The third component in the sale is to know what irritates the different personalities. One of the biggest irritants for a direct, driver style is moving too slowly. If you tend to be methodical, you have a process, and you have eight points you have to hit, and it's going to take a half hour for your presentation with all of this stuff you've prepared, that will irritate a direct, driver person. They'll actually leave somebody in the room and say, "Take the notes. Tell me what's important. I'll be back."

They'll get up and leave a meeting right when you're thinking, "Wait! I'm just getting to the best part." Get to the best part first. Think in terms of a math problem. Give them the answer first, and they will let you know if that answer is important to them. If it's not important to them, move to the next point, be thinking in terms of the Reader's Digest version.

This brings us to the fourth component of making a sale. The best way to communicate or make sales with that direct person is to do your homework first, show up prepared, and follow-up quickly on their questions and on the promises you have made.

The bottom line here is to be brief, be bright, and be gone. Be brief: get to the point. Be bright: make your point brilliant. Be gone: leave them wanting more. I want you to think of stepping into their life and out of their life just like a server at a restaurant. They are a high-end client, and you're touching base with them.

Here's the example I promised you for overcoming an objection if you happen to catch a direct, driver on the phone. If they say, "I don't have time," use words that are in their vocabulary such as, "Okay, great, I get it." Then immediately ask, "Would it be better if I call you back later today or sometime tomorrow?" Now, use caution here because this is an old technique, and if you only ask this either/or question, you know that when you call back, you're just going to get voicemail. In addition, what if you need your question answered today? Then make sure to add a *quick question* prior to ending the conversation with them.

You see, as soon as you've asked that initial question, they know they're getting off the hook, so they say something like, "Probably tomorrow first thing would be great." "All right," you say, "I will do that." Then, before you hang up, throw in that *quick question;* it sounds something like this. "Hey Jo, real quick before we hang up, you said you needed the specs today for your lunch meeting, and I just need a quick answer from you on XYZ to ensure I get you exactly what you need." Or you can say something like, "Okay Sue, I'll call you tomorrow." Then add the *quick question* almost as an afterthought. "Oh, real quick while I've got you on the phone, one short question. I have the specs you requested and wanted to make sure that XYZ is what you needed so I can get that to you immediately before your lunch meeting today. Is this the correct information?" Now you notice in both scenarios the question I needed answered was asked by inserting a *quick question.* By practicing this technique, you will minimize phone tag and stop getting the runaround.

When interacting with direct people they can be more intense, so you needed to dial it up when talking to them. Remember to get to the point, use fewer words, and insert your crucial quick questions. Your tone will change when engaging with the other personality styles.

Let's move now to the thinker-analyzer. Thinker-analyzer types often do not voice their opinions, so dial it down, be methodical and precise. Be accurate and slow things down. What captures their attention is careful analysis and accurate decision making.

Some things that motivate analyzers to purchase include moving at a slower, methodical pace and giving ample time for analysis. Let them know if there are five steps in the process. Let them know the big picture overview. "Here are the five steps; it will take us two weeks to accomplish this. For step 1, we'll do this. In step 2, we'll move to this point, and it should be about three or four days from now. Step 3, we'll move here. That will be by the end of the week. Step 4..."

What analyzers need, is to have that drop-down menu in their head, so as you're selling to this person, be sure to bring things in writing. Thinker-analyzers make a lot of their decisions based on logical deduction, and they love the feature-benefit component. Here's the feature; here's the benefit. More importantly, though, they love the statistics to back it up. They do not make their decisions based on emotion, feeling, or personal opinion. They make them based on the facts.

If you are a natural thinker-analyzer, this will come easily for you. If you are a direct, driver-style person, this will also come easily for you; you'll just have to slow your pace down, be a little bit more detailed, and definitely dial down the intensity.

This can be a challenge for social extroverts who want to jump to different parts and tell what's important to them. That's one of the fastest ways to shut down the sale or irritate the thinker-analyzer.

If you are a relational person, it will be easy for you to match their tone and tempo, the challenge for you is being prepared with the facts and objectives, rather than your feelings or opinions.

Let's go to the hardest part of the sale with the thinker: getting them to commit. One of the things that motivate a thinker-analyzer is doing things right. One of their biggest fears is the fear of looking wrong or doing something wrong or appearing stupid because, from a very young age, they have been rewarded for their intelligence. In a thinker-analyzer's world, they would rather procrastinate on a decision than make a wrong decision.

An irritant during the sale would be offering benefits without telling them the feature, like, "Here's what it will get you. Here's how you can do this." Instead, tell them what the specs are. Tell them the technical side of it because they've probably done their research. Have it in writing, and give it to them. Let them see it. Highlight the parts that are important to them. Let them read it and follow along.

Not knowing your facts is the other irritant in selling to thinkers. If you do not know your facts, please admit it. Let them know. "Hey, you know what,

I don't know that. Let me find out for you." If you can look it up right then and there, great. If you think that's going to be a distraction, tell them you will get back to them. It's really important to the thinker-analyzer that you're doing your homework and that if they request something, you'll get it for them. You can't shoot something off the top of your head and fly off the cuff just to close the sale.

The best techniques for making the sale: provide lots of accurate details—facts, not opinions. Ask lots of either/or questions. Use gentle trial closes to move the sale forward. So instead of getting them to make a big decision, you're getting them to make a series of small decisions. Then using the either/or, "Yes I can do this," or "We can do that," "Which is a higher priority for you? Is it a higher priority to get this done on time? Is this a higher priority for you to get this done under budget? Is it within this budget cycle? Is it a higher priority to have the highest quality?" Be analytical with them. If you're not sure, take cues from them. Listen to what they're asking and then include their words when asking your questions back to them. Bottom line with thinker-analyzers: be prepared, be detailed, take your time, and remember your ABCs. Always be closing.

Let's move now to the social extrovert, innovative, creative-type person. The best way to capture the attention of that socializer is to be fun and creative. Let the fun side of you come out. This is a permission giver for you to come in and have a good time. It is okay to laugh through the process and make sure to allow for some distractions. This kind of thing is okay in your meetings if appropriate, as well as in public settings like restaurants or even on a golf course.

You'll be amazed at how many people can close multi-million dollar deals on the golf course. In fact, I was speaking to my colleague Jeff Wagoner who has been in the corporate world for the majority of his life. Throughout those years, he was blessed with experiencing a lifestyle many of us dream about: one of world travels, corporate jets, private drivers, and residences here and abroad—you get the gist.

Well, Jeff came to a point in his professional career where he thought, "What am I missing in life? What is my purpose here? What am I doing with the rest of my life?" He decided to leave the corporate world in search of what was missing. In the process of finding his own life's calling, he wrote the book *Discover the Unseen* to help other people figure out what's more important to them in their lives.

Bryan, his publisher, said, "You've still got to talk to some of your clients."

Jeff said, "No. I told all my clients I'm not doing this anymore."

Bryan suggested, "Wait a minute here, Jeff. You've got a wealth of knowledge within your clients who want to consult with you and need your help. What if you and your clients agree to the terms of how you consult with them and agree to the understanding that you're gathering information for your book, so, in turn, you can also help other executives break through the barriers that are encountered in the corporate world and help them discover the unseen?"

And so, Jeff went about doing that. Well, on one of his conversations, he was out on the golf course with a friend of a friend who started asking him some questions about the process that Jeff has used to help huge, multi-million dollar corporations become highly functioning corporations at the employee level. Jeff was telling him the process just as they took their 18 holes of golf and this man asked him, "Okay, what would it cost to bring you out to do something like that for my company?"

Now because Jeff had initially decided he was not working the corporate gig anymore, he said, "Well, to coach all of your team and make this work for all of your people for the next year, it's going to take about a year's worth of your time. It's going to be about $500,000."

To Jeff's surprise, the man agreed and shook his hand right there on the golf course. Back at the clubhouse, the guy said, "You know, Jeff, I'm getting a great deal here, $500,000 for what you're going to bring to our company next year. That's amazing. To be perfectly honest with you, I was ready to spend up to $1 million for this."

Jeff believes that the reason the deal closed was because as he puts it "My goal wasn't closing the deal, but helping this person with their business. And since that is what our Lord has instructed us to do—everyone wins in that situation."

Jeff also explained, "I listened to his needs and shared processes (I felt were the best fit) that we had to offer in order to exceed his needs and/or expectations. And those processes not only helped the company and the CEO; they helped everyone working in the company which meant they all had ownership in the newly designed processes. The company had better productivity, the customer received value in the product and services, and my company was paid for our efforts. This was the mindset when I was *socializing*—the deal was real, and I was real. As I said earlier, it's about helping or serving each other so that all benefit. The rest (money) will fall into alignment when your purpose is defined in that way."

"To be genuine, you have to know where you are coming from. Meaning, what is your intention? If my intention was to just *close the deal* and chase the money—that's a different energy that appears and most will see right through it."

The point is that socializers conduct business when they are having fun and being sincere, whether it's a $500,000 deal or a $500 deal. Make it fun and be genuine. Get them engaged. Let them know what the outcome is going to be. Give them that end in mind.

Some of the challenges you'll face in selling to socializers include getting them to stop talking or keeping them on track. Sometimes people are afraid to speak up to socializers because they don't want to interrupt. Yet, realize that from a very young age, social extroverts have been told to get to the point or stay focused. So if you work with or sell to a social extrovert, use those words, something like "Wow! That's a really fascinating story. Let's bring it back to this." Validate the person, give them kudos, and then put them back on track.

Now there are two ways to irritate a social extrovert or a creative person. The first thing is talking about yourself. Social extroverts have a huge WIIFM factor, "I don't need to hear about you unless it has something to do with me." Find out what's important to them. When they're talking, as soon as they take a breath, ask them things like, "How can this product/service help you get you where you want to go? You've talked about your goals, what's stopping you from getting there?" Use open-ended questions that are pointed to help you accomplish your sale.

The second thing that can irritate a socializer is getting lost going down rabbit trails. There are two types of rabbit trails: yours and theirs. We've already talked about your rabbit trails when you're talking, and they're not listening. They don't want to hear your rabbit trail. It's not that they don't care; it's just not relevant to them.

The second rabbit trail is *their* rabbit trail. You might be thinking, "Wait a minute, if it's their rabbit trail, shouldn't I be listening?" Yes, to a point. But if they take a rabbit trail, and you follow them and don't get them back on course, I promise something will interrupt your meeting, and they'll say, "Oh! Where has the time gone? I have another appointment." And you won't get your sale, and you won't be able to pin them down, and they'll often end up buying from a competitor who knows how to work with their style.

The best technique for making the sale is to let them talk. Hone them in on what's important to them. Listen for key features and benefits of what they want. Let them go through the process with you and then reinforce their decision. Ask them about times where they didn't make that decision and what it cost them. I'll give you a personal example of this one. I had put off hiring a professional organizer for many years of my life until my human resources manager asked me what it would do for me to have a professional organizer.

I remember saying to her, "Wow, I could find things. I could get more done in less time. I wouldn't have to feel embarrassed that things were all over the place." *I sold her on why I should hire a professional organizer.*

I give you this illustration to show you, specifically with that socializer style, they have to sell you, the salesperson, because no matter what *you* say, you will not sell them. Instead, make sure you're asking great questions and then let them close you. Then, reinforce their decision by saying things such as, "You're absolutely right. I can see where this is going to help you." Then move them to the next step and give them direction, something like, "Okay, here are our next steps in order to make *that* happen." Or, "Here's what I need you to do. Go ahead and put your name and information here, and I'll get this going over here." At this point, all you're doing is moving to the paperwork stage of the sale. They've already told you they want it. You do not need to ask for it any further. Just put the paperwork in front of them and help them fill it out. Now you can use this technique with all of the styles.

Let's move now to that final style, the relational style. What captures their attention is your level of integrity, your genuineness. They hate hype and love sincerity. When you're speaking with relational people, it is more of a one-on-one conversation. It is about asking a question, letting it sit in the air, and letting them answer it. That is how you capture the attention of relational people; they love a good listener.

What motivates them to purchase is letting them know how their decision is going to free them up to have more time with the things that are important to them in their lives; their family, their friends, the people who are closest to them—time for hobbies, time for volunteering.

Find out what's important to that relational person and they will want to purchase what you have because it will free them up to do what is most important to them. They're *not* motivated by being the coolest, the fastest, or the richest. In fact, if you try to tell them something along those lines, these are relational irritants and will come across as disingenuous, and that relational person will shut you down.

Something that motivates them to purchase is letting them breathe. Present the ideas, then wait a second; hold on a minute. It may take them a while to make a decision, but relational people are some of the best decision makers when they *feel safe and not pressured* because once they say yes, they are true to their word. Their word is their bond. It's a huge part of who they are and their level of integrity.

When I hear a salesperson saying, "I hate selling to relational people, they can't make a decision," what that tells me is this salesperson may need to go back and check their own motives. If you find yourself in a similar situation, ask yourself if you are you selling to them just to get the sale or to enhance their life and, as a result, get the sale.

What motivates that relational person to purchase is knowing that you care. You've heard the motto, "People don't care how much you know until they know how much you care." Relational people know this. Relaters pay attention to the details. They look at your desk and at pictures on the wall. They notice the subtle nuances of the things that are important to you, and they don't point out the obvious—do the same to them.

Make sure that above all else, you are sincere; I'll give you some simple don'ts for selling to relational people based on differing styles.

If you tend to be that thinker-analyzer, and you're selling to a relational person, *don't* come across as being cold and calculating as you present the sterile sales process. It might make logical sense to the relational person; only they won't purchase because they do not purchase on facts. They purchase on how those facts impact their feelings, constantly asking themselves at a gut level, how this is going to affect the people and the lives closest to them.

If you tend to be that direct person, bottom line and to the point, don't use the, "I'm going to push you into a decision" approach or by saying "Come on! Make a decision. I'm going to give you 24 hours to make this decision," you will lose the sale because that relational person says, "No. You cannot push me into the sale." That will kill the sale. That will irritate that relational person. Instead, lead them; persuade them.

If you tend to be that social extrovert who is saying things like, "Hi! We're going to have so much fun! This is going to be a great time. You're going to love this!", you'll come across as disingenuous. In the example I used of Jeff on the golf course, he was able to be relational because he was real and genuine with a direct socializer style and move through a golf course while adapting to a direct, bottom line-type style and in the process, closing the deal.

Relational people can be sold to and can be great salespeople if you understand what motivates them as well as what irritates them.

Relational people with analytical undertones are very respectful of your time and their own time. Let them know the process in that analytical order like you do with the pure thinker-analyzer and, at the same time, let them know the feelings associated with it and that you will be asking them to be making decisions throughout the process. It's the same technique you use with that thinker-analyzer ABC, always be closing.

It is a similar technique that you use with the social extrovert of asking them what this is going to do for them, how it will free up their time, and how in turn they can benefit from it. When you use these techniques, they work. The level of truthfulness that you bring to the table ensures that they will work on a genuine level.

You had some time to think about your personality style and the different styles of people that you sell to. I want to move you to the next secret, which is reviewing where you are in your competency level, as well as where your prospective clients are in their competency levels.

Bottom line. If you want to successfully sell to different female personalities, then adapt and adjust your style to theirs. Just like traveling to a foreign country, learn enough of the language that they speak; emulate their tone, tempo and body language and do your best to find common ground to build on. If she is a direct, bottom line and to the point person, assertively be the same back with her. If she is a thinker-analyzer, come prepared with the facts and data and expect to field many technical and hypothetical questions. If she's a social extrovert, have fun, expect rabbit trails and ask great questions to get her back on track. If she's a relational person, be a sincere listener, genuine in your questions and patient in the process, give deadlines, but don't force them.

Chapter 7

The Four Stages of Competency

Knowing where you are in your competency level of understanding your audience, the person you're selling to, and even yourself, is the final technique in this book and the first step to building skill.

Now the first key to understanding the four stages of competency is recognizing where you are in your competency level based on what you've been practicing. As stated earlier, practice makes permanent. You and your life have been built on a series of repeated thoughts and habits—including your selling habits. There might be some areas when it comes to selling to people where you're really, really good. Maybe you're good at initiating that first call or the follow-up call, or the face-to-face selling, or maybe you're really good with the paperwork and making sure everything is in order. Maybe you're great at connecting with people and making them feel valued and cherished, or maybe you're good at just getting along with people.

Yet there are parts of the sales process that just don't come together for you. What I want you to think about as I discuss the four stages of competencies is where you are in the different stages of your life, and where your clients are in their understanding of what you're trying to sell them.

Stage 1: Unconscious Incompetence. This is where you don't know what you don't know, and you don't know that you don't know it. Name an area in your life where you are unconsciously incompetent. It's a trick question. You can't name something you don't know that you don't know because...you don't know it! These are your blind spots. Think of someone who has a quirky tendency they are not aware of; maybe they stick their tongue out when they are typing on the computer keyboard. Everyone who has ever walked by them knows about it, but they themselves are unaware. What if there are things you naturally do as part of the sales process that hinders your chances of making sales to women, wouldn't you want to become aware of them?

I liken this to when you used to be a passenger in a car. Remember when you knew nothing about the rules of the road, and you just needed to get to from point A to point B? You didn't understand how it felt to hydroplane on a puddle; you had no idea how to adjust your speed to stay on the road through a hairpin curve. You may have even complained to the driver about how they were doing it. You were unaware that you did not know how to parallel park until you became consciously aware of that incompetence, which is stage two.

Stage 2: Conscious Incompetence. This is where you get, what I like to say, the *wake-up call*. You now know there is something you don't know that you didn't know. Just as important, you know everybody around you knows that you don't know it. Welcome to the wake-up call. With conscious incompetence, it's embarrassing when you realize you don't know something you didn't know, just like in the car situation, you remember all the things you said to the driver that were totally out of line.

Like when you had to learn to parallel park the car. Now, you may have practiced before you ever took driver's education, but for the rest of us, it was that awkward moment of having to put the car in reverse, then put it back in drive, put the car in reverse, put it back in drive. How many times did you jerk the car back and forth until you finally got into that space or worse, your driver's education teacher said, "Never mind. We'll come back to this later."

When you have that wake-up call, and you realize you're incompetent at something, one of two things is going to happen. You're either going to embrace it and do what it's going to take to change and become competent in that area or you're going to rationalize, justify, and excuse why you can't change.

I want to go back to Stephen Covey here for just a moment. He says, "A person will live aware of their incompetency for 21 to 30 years, to 40 years, to 50 years, to life because they don't know how to change, or they're afraid to change, or they just don't want to change." Here's what it sounds like. You can tell when somebody is at a stage of conscious incompetence when they say things like this: "Well, this is just who I am." "You know you can't teach an old dog new tricks." "You've heard about the good, the bad, and the ugly; this is just a little bit of ugly." "Guess what, I'm not perfect." or "It's not my skillset." The truth is, anytime we say something like that to ourselves in an area that we know we're incompetent in, we're stopping ourselves from moving forward.

I mentioned earlier that my human resource manager said to me, "Dawn, have you thought about hiring a professional organizer?" Let me give you, as famous broadcaster Paul Harvey would say, "The rest of the story" on that one. Here I am, co-founder and president of a safety training company in Seattle, and I hire the human resource manager to help keep us in compliance and manage our HR issues. Well, I have an expectation that my employees are going to leave the workplace at the end of the day with their desks clean. If I need to find something, I'll be able to find it, be it at their desk, at their workstation, on the computer, wherever it might be. I had this (unofficial) rule that I needed to be able to find it within 30 seconds, and if I couldn't find it, then you weren't organized.

The biggest problem was I couldn't find stuff in my own workstation. I had developed what I called clutter piles. That's just a nice way of saying I had messy piles of paperwork on my desk. Here was the challenge with my little clutter piles. First of all, I had given them a name. Second of all, I had reinforced why it was okay to have those little clutter piles on my desk. I would say things to myself such as, "Please don't straighten out the mess in my workstation. You'll confuse me and screw up my whole world." Or I would see little placards that said things like, "A Clean Desk is a Sign of an Empty Mind," and I would think, "That's a good one to put on my desk." Secretly I even liked that bumper sticker that said: "Always late, but worth the wait!"

I had these rationalizations that I would use to excuse my behavior; I would say, "Oh, I'm just really creative," or, "I know where everything is." The actuality is I was lying to myself because I didn't know how to change, and worse, I was afraid that if somebody showed me how to change, it wouldn't work for me. So I put up with being highly disorganized and highly creative for over fifteen years of my adult life until my human resource manager came in and gave me the wake-up call when she was asking for a check to pay the State of Washington for our business license.

On the scale of life, it was a small check. It wasn't a big deal, yet I couldn't find it for her, and I couldn't find it the second time she came back. And so when she came back the third time, I wrote another check. A few weeks later, I found the first check in the clutter pile.

They say awareness of the problem is the first step to fixing it, but remember the pain of not changing must become greater than the pain of changing before most of us will take action. I use this as an illustration because many of us get stuck in phases in our lives that could so easily be changed if we just chose to go to stage three, and that is conscious competence.

Stage 3: Conscious Competence. This is where you take the *wake-up call*, identify what needs to be changed, and implement the steps to change it. You've probably heard somewhere in your life that it takes 21 days to change a thought and 30 days to change a behavior. Here's the caveat: *if practiced with intensity*. If you practice that change over the 21 to 30-day time period with intensity—and that means learning a new way to do something, practicing it, maybe feeling a little bit embarrassed, feeling a little bit foolish, or even frustrated not knowing how to do it perfectly but still sticking with it—that's when you see lasting and permanent change, and that's what I mean by practicing with intensity. I'm going to give you a simple illustration of this.

If you're able to, take a moment, stop what you're doing, and sign your name on a piece of paper. Yes, any piece of paper, even scrap paper will do; and yes, sign right now with a pen or a pencil, it doesn't matter, just write it like you've been signing it for years. Now stop and look at your signature you wrote. You've practiced it. It looks good. Now, I'm guessing you did that effortlessly. Here is a simple example of something you've practiced doing so long that you can do it without thinking. Now I want you to do something I learned from another author, Debra Fox. Take the pen or pencil and move it from your dominant writing hand to your non-dominant writing hand. Just move it over. Yes, right now. Okay, freeze. Don't do anything else. When I do this in my talks, training courses, and coaching sessions, 99 percent of the time, almost everybody has moved the pen over to the other hand but not without letting out a grunt, "ugh" or rolling their eyes because they have to move from something they're comfortable with to something they're uncomfortable with.

I want you to think about that "ugh" sound because anytime you are making a change in your life, your brain is going to give you that sound. It might not be audible, yet you will hear it in your head, and I want you to embrace that sound as the sound of change. All I did was ask you to move the pen from one hand to the other. You made the change. You just moved the pen over. Yet you likely groaned in the process.

Let's talk about the *why* behind that groan. Let's talk about what you were thinking. What were some fears or inconveniences that were in your head when I asked you to make that change? Like, "Maybe she's going to ask me to sign my name with my other hand." That's the big one. I didn't ask you to write anything, did I? No. Yet that was the fear. And so, the fear or inconvenience is a fear of the unexpected or the unknown of what's going to happen next; and if you have to write your name with your other hand, it's not going to look as nice as your practiced signature.

What does this exercise have to do with assessing your competency level? Everything. You see, as you're moving through the stages of competency, realize there are some areas where you might be unconsciously incompetent. Somebody might come in and give you a wake-up call. It might be a nice wake-up call like I received from my human resources manager, or it might be an embarrassing wake-up call where you feel exposed and vulnerable in front of a whole bunch of people. At that pivotal point, you can rationalize, justify, and excuse your behavior for 21 to 30 years—to life *or* you can embrace the wake-up call and practice for 21 to 30 days a new habit or new behavior. Embrace the change.

Recognize the sound of change. Recognize the feelings, and then find someone or something to get you from where you are to where you want to go. In my case, when my human resource manager came back in the third time she said, "Dawn, have you thought about hiring a professional organizer?"

I had all sorts of obstacles. I didn't think I could afford it. I didn't have the time. No, I would just give up and go back to my old systems. Those are my tales of woe for being consciously incompetent when it came to being organized. You'll recognize yours. Also, recognize your customers'. Any time you're asking for the sale, you're asking your potential customer to change the pen to the other hand. In my circumstance, my human resources manager came prepared, and even though she was not a salesperson, she had to sell me an idea in order to do her job better. You see, my organization skills (or lack thereof) were her obstacle. And if we had both been men, all she would have needed to do was help me see it as an obstacle, and we would have rallied around clearing it in an expedient, straight-line, left-brain sort of way. But as women, we needed to build consensus and consider all the consequences before forming a plan of action.

So if she had just come in and told me, "Dawn, you need to do this, so I can do my job better," it wouldn't have caught my attention. Instead, she said, "Dawn, imagine what a professional organizer could do for you. She could bring you systems. You could have a place for everything, and everything would have its place. You'd be able to find things in less time. You wouldn't have to do duplicate work."

This woman was prepared. I don't know how much time she thought about this, but it must have been a long time because her job was not sales and she came in and sold me as to why I should hire a professional organizer. Then she took it a step further. She went through my list of clients and said, "Dawn, I'm noticing here, you have a professional organizer as one of your clients, and I know she needs some business coaching. What if you made a trade with her? You help her with her sales and with her business and increasing her bottom line and building her confidence while she helps you get organized."

As I looked back over the situation, the technique that she unconsciously used was to *sell to me as a woman*. I realized it was very, very different than selling to a man.

Statistically, men will fail more because they take more risks. Women, on the other hand, believe the converse to be true, thinking they will succeed more because they take fewer risks—at least, it looks that way.

Here's the reality though: because men fail more, they succeed more overall and oftentimes women don't step out because they're afraid of failing. So while women fail less, they also risk less and, therefore, succeed less overall. Women often ask, "What will people think?" They risk less due to the fear of being judged by other people for not following cultural norms. On a hormonal level, men have more testosterone than women, which causes men to risk more while women have more estrogen which causes them to be more cautious and risk less.

When you are specifically selling to a woman, make sure you factor that in. This is not about positioning, and circumstance, and achievement, and accomplishment. This is about getting to the core of who that woman is so that she can break the habit she has lived with for years. When you give that wake-up call, you do it in a way that's for her benefit even if you're going to benefit from it as well—that's when you'll see the beginning of change. Because here, my human resource manager was going to benefit from all of the things I could learn from a professional organizer, yet I listened because of how it would set me free with something I had struggled with for so many years.

When I spoke with the organizer, here was the irony. We had a phone consultation and she asked me a series of questions. As I described my office to her, I described the challenges that I was having, and she said to me, "I think we could probably fix this in a Saturday." I thought to myself. "No, no, no. You haven't seen my office."

She said, "Why don't we just do our initial consultation. I'll come out to your office. We'll do it on a Saturday. None of your staff will be there." Again, pay attention here on this one: another selling feature. The professional organizer knew I was the president of the company. And so, rather than do this when I had staff around, she said, "Let me come to your office on a weekend. Let's take four hours at a time. Let's develop a system and let's set you on the path to success," and that's exactly what she did.

Another irony: she gets to my office, looks around and says, "Oh! We can definitely get this done this Saturday in four hours."

Now at that moment, I'm thinking to myself, "Wait a minute! Is she pulling my leg here or is she just trying to get the sale? She's already got the sale." That cynical side of me kind of wonders why is she using this technique, so I ask for more information.

She says, "Dawn, your office is an easy fix. I have gone into people's offices where they have books and papers and files stacked three to four feet high with just a path to their desks."

Next, she says to me, "Dawn, here's what we're going to do. I'm going to set you up with some systems. I'm going to walk you through those systems today and then everything you put somewhere in your office is going to go to one of three places."

Now if this is something that you personally struggle with, just a sidebar here, you might want to write this down. Everything in your life goes to one of three places, and here's how she explains it, "Dawn, you're going to **keep it,** or you're going to **toss it**, or you're going to **file it."**

I say, "Okay, keep it, toss it, file it. I got it. I can do that."

She continues, "Here's how you figure out if you're going to keep it, toss it, or file it.

Keep it: the questions are where and why. Where are you going to keep it and why do you need to keep it? In fact, let's cover the why first. Do you really need to keep it?"

She used the example of an executive who had a three-hole punch on her desk. There's no reason why an executive should have a three-hole punch. It has to "earn a place on your workstation."

Not only was she teaching me techniques for getting organized, but she was also teaching me techniques for delegating and not trying to do everything. Here I am hiring this professional organizer, and she's helping me become a better leader.

She even went as far as bringing me a little, organized tray that had pictures in there of where the stapler went, of where the tape went, of where the pencils went. I know that seems a little bit elementary. Yet, realize the skills I had at the age of 35 in this area were elementary. I was unconsciously incompetent, and she had to take me through that breakpoint, or blind spot.

I still use organizers to this day. The pictures are long gone. The organizers have been updated. My desk has been upgraded and rearranged. Yet those were fundamentals that I needed.

"Toss it," she goes on. "You toss it into the recycle bin, to the shredder, or the trash can, or to another person. That's introducing delegation."

For **file it,** she gave me a system for filing, which, I customized over the years to meet my needs, made it my own, and then I put into my *Taking Control of Time and Priorities* audio.

The thing here, though, is she gave me systems. She gave me the day to practice putting them into place. A habit can be changed overnight if you have a method to follow. You practice it for 21 to 30 days with intensity, like we covered earlier, until it becomes a habit that you do effortlessly.

In that 21 to 30-day time, she followed up with a couple of phone calls and suggested that I read and listen to things that helped me stay organized.

I was in a seminar and picked up a few time management audio learning programs. One on how to organize your life, another on how to delegate work, and another on controlling your workday. Instead of hearing my own thoughts in my head while I was cleaning my workstation, I listened to those audios and they changed the way I thought about getting organized.

Here was something else I had learned so many years before from a Tony Robbins seminar. He said, "If you want to be good at something, learn how to do it. You don't have to reinvent the wheel. Learn from somebody who is successfully doing it. If you want to get better at something, continue to do it repeatedly. Do that until it becomes a habit. If you want to master it, teach other people how to do it." Tony also said that if you want to remain the best at what you have mastered, you must go back to basics and continue to keep your skills sharp— listen to, watch, read, and engage kinesthetically with it. That moves us into unconscious competence.

Stage 4: Unconscious Competence. This is where you're just doing things naturally without thinking—you have formed great habits for life. You've gone through the processes of stages one and two from being unconscious to consciously aware of your incompetence. Then moving into the challenging and exhilarating stage three, you consciously choose to become competent and move in a new direction; choosing to think differently, to act differently and learn from other people who have gone before you in those very same areas. Those others have left a path for you to follow so that you too could achieve the highest level of success with integrity in an area you thought could never change. Moving through these stages so that you could reach the pinnacle of mastery, you become unconsciously competent in something that was just a dream at one time in your life. If you had told me when I was 35 years old, "Dawn, if you hire a professional organizer, you will take control of your time and your priorities and get organized and be more accomplished, get more things done, have higher quality time, have improved relationships, and be less stressed." I would have thought that was great.

If you had told me that, in addition to those things, I would become a published author and speaker paid to travel internationally and teach other people how to take control of their time and priorities and find more satisfaction in work and life, I would have said that's not possible because I knew how much I had struggled in these areas. This is the power of understanding where we are in our competency levels. When you understand where you are in your level of competency, you can invite the wake-up call and listen to, watch, participate in, or be coached through the process of becoming unconsciously competent. I am truly grateful that I have had the privilege of traveling to many parts of the world to coach, train, and help people grow in their competence and live more fulfilling lives.

Also by recording internationally distributed audio training programs that people use as tools for getting unstuck, I now have the privilege of helping listeners organize their time and priorities in work and life rather than being stuck for 21-30 years. *Taking Control of Time and Priorities* and *Organizing your Work and Life* are top-selling resources; I am truly grateful and amazed. Not only is it possible, but it's totally doable if you are willing to embrace that sound of change. Put the pen in the other hand, follow some instructions, and as Nike says, "Just Do It." That is the power of understanding the four stages of competency.

Remember the Deloitte consultants who lost the contract in our introduction? They decided to move from conscious incompetence to unconscious competence, so they made learning how to sell to women a part of their management team's training and development curriculum. So, if you are a senior manager undergoing this training, you work on a simulated proposal for a client, interacting with actors trained to play the part of client executives.

They look for what you noticed. Do you absorb the staged clues about the female client: the books on her shelf, the magazine on the table, the picture on her desk? Do you establish a rapport by commenting on those things, such as the people or settings in her photos, in your initial greeting? Do you mirror and match her personality style and integrate her learning modality? If she says she likes your tie, do you simply say "thanks" or do you tell the story of how you happened to buy it? She wants to know about the person she will be working with, and your usual approach might not reveal that kind of information.

During training sessions, the failure to establish rapport is the most frequent mistake male professionals make. In most cases, the male team members go directly to the purpose of the meeting and work through their content agenda. They may be unaware that the female client sees the meeting as a way to get to know the people she is being asked to trust with her business. Or they may not know how to respond to that objective. So the listening challenge is to discover what she wants to achieve and what she feels is the most comfortable way to do so. A good place to start is to use the time it takes to get settled in her office to strike up a conversation and establish rapport.

In her meeting with you, the female executive is aware of you as a knowledgeable resource on her organization's problem and a useful sounding board for novel ideas. She is also sizing you up as a creative collaborator. If she deviates from the line of thinking you are presenting, do you go with the flow or try to force the conversation back to your agenda? The key is to watch and listen for clues that your client is engaged in a discovery process and adapt your behavior and style accordingly. Be nimble and prepared to shift from what you rehearsed, then practice until it becomes habitual[19].

Deloitte says, "Training our presenters to examine and adjust their habitual behaviors has value beyond gender situations. Our partners and managers have improved their emotional intelligence and their ability to deal empathetically with all prospects and clients (and with teammates and family members). In teaching men how to sell to women, we're really teaching them how to understand people as individuals. And we're reinforcing the importance of respecting diversity in our internal interactions—a win all around."

Bottom Line. When you are open to growing and developing in your competency blind spots, you will discover more purpose and fulfillment in work and life.

BONUS

Confidence in Selling to Women

Keep in mind that selling to women includes being confident. Now this is not to be confused with being cocky or arrogant, or *faking it until you make it*. This is just being confident. Coming in knowing that you are listening, you are prepared to learn, and you are also prepared to teach your client what they need. Whether you are displaying this confidence over the phone, or over the Internet, face-to-face, or when sending emails and correspondences, being confident is essential when it comes to successfully selling to a woman and making a living from your talent.

Confidence comes across in four ways including: your voice, your words, your facial expressions, and your credibility. Let's briefly go over them one at a time starting with your voice.

Voice. Your voice should be melodic yet professional. Think about it. People get voicemails all day long that sound drab or annoying. Those messages can be spoken at monotone levels that sound as though the person who is leaving the message is completely bored, or they can sound whiny as though they're in chronic pain. Or they sound really hyper as though they've had four shots of espresso before calling you. Or they can sound as though the caller has no brains whatsoever. You get the picture. Let your voice be warm, melodic, intentional, and professional.

Words. Your voice says more than your words. Though words are important, it's how you say those words that make all the difference, which brings us to the second element in being confident on the phone and that's the words you use, or should I say the words you choose.

Being prepared in your presentation is key when it comes to successfully selling to women. This includes writing out and practicing what you're going to say before you ever pick up the phone or make the sales call. Apply the principles of asking great questions because remember; practice makes permanent, and you always sound more confident when you are prepared.

When making calls, always include why you're calling. Be specific, because even if you reach someone who's too busy to take your call right now, you can still leave a quick question or two in their voicemail, or an instant message, or an email that keeps that phone tag or those emails to a minimum.

Facial Expressions. The third element in boosting your confidence includes your facial expressions because what's not being said is being heard. Smile when you speak, especially on the phone. How much better is it when you get a voicemail that sounds as though the person who's leaving the message is actually looking forward to speaking with you?

Contributing author Sherry Prindle can attest to the auditory power of the smile. She puts it this way, "I lived in Moscow, Russia for three years and got a job doing the news in English at the bottom of every hour on a Russian radio station. I imagined the Russian listeners were irritated by this interruption by a foreign language, but on the contrary, I began receiving abundant fan letters, faxes, and calls. We assumed the fans spoke English, but when we inquired, we found that most of them did not understand a word I was saying. The consensus was that they enjoyed hearing my "smiling, sparkling voice."" Now that's what I call a powerful smile!

The same goes when you're trying to reach another person, be sincere, and smile. Ask great questions. Though this may seem elementary, it is surprising how many people are unprepared when they pick up the phone.

So, I want to give you an action item right now. Take a moment to leave yourself a voicemail on your own phone. Pretend you're making a sales call to yourself. Leave the message and then go back and listen to it. As you play it back, listen to see if you sound like somebody that you would like to call back or somebody you'd like to delete. Then practice changing the above-mentioned items until your voice is natural and enjoyable to listen to.

Body Language. Please note that women's body language does not mean the same things that men's does. For example, men often nod when something the speaker has said is familiar to them, or they agree and they want the discussion to move on; whereas women tend to nod to signal interest in what is being said and to encourage the speaker to elaborate. This often throws salespeople for a loop. The potential female client nods throughout the whole presentation but declines the offer.

While a male client might prefer sitting next to a consultant to confer about something, women more often choose a seat across the table, wanting to speak face-to-face. In fact, women generally talk face-to-face while men stand side-by-side. Start noticing the subtleties of the most important aspect of communication, nonverbal.

Listening. Men listen for facts and figures, often more focused on getting the best deal. Women want the complete story and are more interested in learning about quality and getting the right product or service to suit their needs. With women, learn to listen with your ears, eyes, and feelings to pick up on all the dimensions they are bringing to the communication.

One other common misinterpretation comes in the form of an apology. Males tend to view an apology as a confession of responsibility, whereas women are "sorry" the other person has had a negative experience completely independently from having any fault in the matter.

Women see a big meeting with a potential service provider as a chance to explore options in collaboration with an expert resource while men see that event as a near-final step in the process. Men tend to end a conversation once they connect with a good idea or solution while women are inclined to be more inquisitive, wanting to hear everyone's thoughts before deciding.

Credibility. The final element of being confident when selling to women is your credibility. Being credible allows the person you're connecting with to start building trust with you. Once trust is established in any relationship, there is a certain amount of natural confidence that comes with it. When you deliver what you promise, whether it's in an email or return phone call, or sending out your information packet, the woman who is considering buying from you is unconsciously or *technically* subconsciously watching to see if you are reliable. The more reliable you are, the more that woman will trust you. When trust is achieved and maintained, you've established your credibility and greatly improved your chances of making the sale.

When it comes to being confident while selling to women, remember to practice what you've learned today. Establish some good habits and practice your sales presentation.

Keep in mind the four essentials we've just covered. Speak with a melodic, professional voice. Choose the right words with great questions. Remember your facial expressions and smile when you speak and demonstrate your credibility by delivering what you promise.

When you practice and apply these good habits, increased confidence is a natural result because by implementing these tips, techniques, and tools that we've gone over in this program, you can confidently do what you fear most and the death of fear is certain, which brings us back to selling to women and why women buy.

Bottom line, when you're selling specifically to a woman, remember *Chapter 1: Recognize How Women Differ from Men* and that it is okay to acknowledge and welcome those differences. Allow these differences into your sales process. Remember to accentuate the positive differences and create a win-win situation. Then utilize the motivation that comes from *Chapter 2: Overcome the Fear of Sales.* Face your sales fears, learn from great salespeople and implement those techniques into your work and life. Then, take that know-how and help your clients break free from the things holding them back. Use leverage, and vision to keep your goals and your clients' goals at the forefront of your sales intentions giving you the motivation to go after the sale and have greater confidence when selling to women.

Chapter 3: Operate with Integrity. Some tips you can use to keep this in mind is to be the person that you expect her to be—be that person of integrity. Deliver what you say. Exceed her expectations. Be the same person publicly, privately, and secretly. This is not about just closing the sale. This is about establishing a relationship, and whether it is a short-term relationship or a long-term relationship, your integrity comes through. She can sense whether you are or are not genuine; it can be something subtle, like the twitch of an eye. It can be how you're looking at her in the conversation. It can be in your presentation when you know what you're talking about versus when you might be winging it. She may not be an expert on human psychology, but just like you, she is an expert on human behavior, and it is in those subtle nuances that she determines if you are a person of integrity or not. Practice being the person that you say that you are because practice makes permanent, which ties into *Chapter 4: Ask Great Questions.* Remember, *yes* and *no* questions are red, to remind you to stop and think before you ask those questions and to remind you to look for an agreeable answer. *Open-ended questions* are yellow, to remind you to use caution when asking so that you don't stump your listener or enter into lengthy answers, but rather ask the questions that give you the information you're looking for. *Either/or* questions are blue like the ocean, to remind you that when you include multiple choice options, blend your questions to keep the conversation flowing. Periodically repeat her questions back to her using backtracking and rhetorical questions. Incorporate hypothetical questions and use pre-calling questions to overcome objections in advance. Be consistent and persistent, listening to what she needs and being easy to work with.

Chapter 5: Integrate All Four Communication Styles. This is the key to engagement, Read her quickly. Understand her preferred learning method. Does she want the facts? Does she want to see things in writing? Does she need to hear them? Does she want a visual? Is she more kinesthetic? Understand her. What does she need? Then adapt your sales style to meet her needs, remember the WIIFM factor, what's in it for her, not necessarily for you as the salesperson.

Then factor in *Chapter 6: Selling to the Different Personality Types.* Take time to understand what her personality style is. Is she that bottom-line, decisive driver, or that linear, logical thinker/analyzer, or maybe she's that creative, expressive social extrovert, or perhaps she's that quiet and patient relational person.

When you're speaking to her, match her style. And remember, if you don't know which style she is? Ask her a question. You can tell a lot by how she answers. Ask her an open-ended question like, "What is most important to you in purchasing this product?" or "What would be the most important thing that you want to make sure that you get from this?" Listen for whether she stays big-picture or gets into detail and whether she is direct or indirect. Does she talk about facts or about feelings?

Get to the point if she's a driver; a driver is going to say something like, "I want to get things done. I need you to…"

You can hear the tone and the tempo in her voice tell you this is a bottom-line, to-the-point, no-nonsense, "Give me what I need so I can get on with my day" kind of person.

If you are speaking to that analyzer and you ask that same question, she may give you a list of things and tell you why it's important and what the research shows and she wants to know that this isn't going to be something that's going to become obsolete in two years or five years from now. She is going to be quoting facts and statistics to you. Make sure you adapt your style to her; this is not about her adapting her style to you.

With the personality style of the social extrovert, that creative person, you can know right off the bat by how they multitask—if they can jump from one conversation to another. This is about you matching and mirroring their style and then leading them where you need them to go. Be prepared with your questions. Know that you're going to interject with that conversation and move them from a starting point to a finish line.

Then when you're speaking with the relational person, the relational style encompasses the traditional style of a woman raised to be caring, considerate, and nurturing. So be caring, be considerate, be nurturing. Be those things. You are matching and mirroring that person and in addition, you are the person that you say you are.

Then, when you're selling specifically to women, remember to keep in mind *Chapter 7: The Four Stages of Competency.* Factor in where you and she are in the stages of competency. If you're comfortable with her, you've established a great rapport, and you're thinking to yourself something along the lines of, "You know, I could *unconsciously competently* walk through the sales process with her because I believe I understand how she thinks and what she wants," then this will be an easy sale for both of you. On the other hand, maybe you're thinking, "This is a challenging person for me. This is the sale that I usually don't get. This is the one I dismiss because they don't make a decision or they're hard to deal with, they're just too wishy-washy." If you find yourself saying things like that, ask yourself where you are in your stage of competency in dealing with this person, and what it is going to take to become consciously competent with them so that you can make that sale with them.

Then reinforce your good habits. It takes 21 days to change a thought, 30 days to change a habit; this is nothing new. What is new, and what I'm hoping that you're taking away from this, is the caveat of *if you practice with intensity*. If you practice with intensity, whatever happens in your sales processes that you're challenged with, listen to the Zig Ziglars, listen to the Brian Tracys, listen to the Chris Wideners, listen to and read the programs like you're learning from right now to help you become the person you want to be and break those old habits. By just listening to, and reviewing something you have learned six to ten times, you can quickly become the expert.

As stated earlier, if you want to get good at something, learn how to do it. If you want to master it, teach other people how to do it, which is exactly what you're doing in the sales process.

Closing Thoughts

I hope you enjoyed our time together and learned some tips, techniques, and secrets to help you effectively sell to women. I want to leave you with some encouraging people from history who mastered the very things you've been reading about and, as a result, changed the world in which we live. These people recognized the importance of communicating their message, without fear and with integrity to a variety of personality types—both men and women—while factoring in the best communication modalities and while asking great questions—questions that caused people to think, questions that persuaded people to change their hearts and minds—these people changed the way we live today.

Dr. Martin Luther King Jr. had such an impact on society that with his dream, he exposed the unjust division of our nation and influenced thousands of people to take action by embracing his vision and passion as their own. His passion was born out of the unjust treatment of one people group to another. Though he's most remembered for his famous "I have a dream" speech, the incident that brought him national recognition was the 1955-56 Alabama bus boycott, which led to the arrest of a black woman named Rosa Parks for her refusal to give up her seat on a city bus to a white man! Dr. King Jr. took a stand against injustice and changed the face of the United States!

Another man who has made an impact on society is Mahatma Gandhi. In one of his last notes left behind in 1948 he wrote: "...Whenever you are in doubt, or when the self becomes too much with you, apply the following test: Recall the face of the poorest and weakest man whom you have seen and ask yourself if the step you contemplate is going to be of any use to him. Will he gain anything by it? Will it restore him to a control over his own life and destiny? In other words, will it lead to freedom for the hungry and spiritually starving millions? Then you will find your doubts and yourself melt away."[20]

What about Mother Theresa? She devoted herself to working among the poorest of the poor in the slums of Calcutta. According to her biography, "Although she had no funds, she depended on Divine Providence and started an open-air school for slum children. Soon she was joined by voluntary helpers, and financial support was also forthcoming. This made it possible for her to extend the scope of her work."[21]

Then there is a man who radically changed the world of his day along with our modern world, Jesus Christ. His simple message of turning away from selfish desire, loving others as yourself and putting God first has given millions of people around the world hope and purpose. Another interesting fact about Jesus is that he is truly the dividing point of our world history. Regardless of what you believe, Jesus impacted the world so much that until the 1980's the world's calendar was regulated by his life and death (AD and BC, now more commonly referred to as CE and BCE). These examples show that just one person can make a difference even to the point of altering the course of history and time!

When it comes to implementing the selling to women techniques into your life, remember that sales people come and go. Therefore, sell with integrity because a good name is far better than ill-gained wealth. Sell without fear by using your gifts and talents to influence people for good. Choose to sell things that will leave this world a better place. And sell remembering that at the end of your days, what you leave behind on this Earth is the legacy you leave behind forever—one person *can* change the world!

Watch your thoughts; they become your words. Watch your words; they become your actions. Watch your actions; they become your habits or behaviors. Watch your habits and behaviors because they become your character, and watch your character because it's who you've become.

About the Author

Dawn Jones is an international speaker, certified coach, corporate trainer, and **best-selling author** of the *Top 7 Personality Challenges*. For more than 20-years, Dawn Jones has empowered over 50,000 people in more than 1,200 presentations, in 8 countries. Whether she is working with Leaders, Project Managers, Sales People, or Entrepreneurs, Dawn is passionate about helping people achieve their goals!

For over 5-years she's been in the top 1% of salespeople for her clients in the corporate training industry and holds the record for highest sales day in the 25-year history of one of her top clients. Her perseverance, passion, and spontaneous humor stem from over 20 years as an entrepreneur, professional business owner, volunteer, and wife.

Dawn's fast-paced delivery, sprinkled with impacting stories and anecdotes, makes her one of the most stimulating and sought-after speaker/authors in her specialty areas. Dawn addresses eager audiences both LIVE, and on audio, in books, and on DVD. Her corporate travels have taken her to Australia, New Zealand, England, and across North America. Her recently published recordings include *Taking Control of Time and Priorities*; *Dealing with Difficult People*; *How to Supervise People*; *Conflict Management Skills for Women*; *What is Leadership*? *What is Success*? As well as compilations with Zig Ziglar, Brian Tracy, Chris Widener, and Les Brown.

More than a theorist, Dawn has put her insights and methods to the test over and over in real-life situations, both professionally and personally. Her techniques are easy to implement. They work. And when combined, they create a concrete road map that helps people to triumph over obstacles in their life and achieve their goals.

In her free time, Dawn travels with her husband to Africa where they volunteer with non-profit groups to help build a hope and a future for the next generation.

You can contact Dawn at dawnjones.net or 1.877.686.1955.

Notes

1. Nanette Fondas and Susan Sassalos, "A Different Voice in the Boardroom: How the Presence of Women Directors Affects Board Influence Over Management", *Global Focus* Volume 12, Issue 2 (2000), pp. 13-22.

2. Cathy Benko and Bill Pelster, "How Women Decide" *Harvard Business Review,* September 2013, https://hbr.org/2013/09/how-women-decide.

3. Gabe Rosenberg, "Study: 91 Percent of Women Feel Misunderstood by Advertisers" *Contently.* July 1, 2014, https://contently.com/strategist/2014/07/01/study-91-percent-of-women-feel-misunderstood-by-advertisers.

4. Faith Popcorn and Lys Marigold, *Eveolution: Understanding Women--Eight Essential Truths That Work in Your Business and Your Life* (New York: Hachette Books, 2001).

5. Christine Gorman, "Sizing up the Sexes," *TIME Magazine,* January 1992, 36–43.

6. Pat Brennan, "UCI Researcher: Male, Female Brains are Different 'Mosaics'", *Orange County Register,* August 21, 2013, http://www.ocregister.com/articles/differences-382702-women-male.html.

7. Gina Kolata, "Men and Women Use Brain Differently, Study Discovers", *New York Times, February 16, 1995.*

8. Diane Carlson Jones, *Developmental Psychology* 40, no. 5 (Sep 2004): 823-835.

9. Pat Heim and Susan K. Golant, *Hardball for Women: Revised Edition*, 2nd ed. (New York: Plume, 2005).

10. Susan Heitler, PhD, "How Gender Differences Make Decision-Making Difficulties" *Psychology Today*, February 2, 2012, https://www.psychologytoday.com/blog/resolution-not-conflict/201202/how-gender-differences-make-decision-making-difficulties.

11. Benko and Pelster, "How Women Decide." *Harvard Business Review,* September 2013.

12. Susan Vinnicombe et al., ed., *Women in Corporate Boards of Directors International Research and Practice* (Northampton: Edward Elgar Publishing, 2008)

13. Ilan Shrira, "Women More Likely Than Men to See Nuance When Making Decisions", *Scientific American*, September 20, 2011, http://www.scientificamerican.com/article/sex-roles-and-seeing-the-world-in-black-and-white.

14. Colin F. Camerer, California Institute of Technology 2003.

15. Chris Bart and Gregory McQueen, "Why Women Make Better Directors" *International Journal of Business Governance and Ethics 8*, no. 1 (2013): 93-99.

16. Benko and Pelster "How Women Decide." *Harvard Business Review*, September 2013.

17. Kelsey Libert, "Age and Gender Matter in Viral Marketing" *Harvard Business Review*, August 18, 2014.

18. Kit Barmann, "Purchasing Power of Women," *FONA International*, December 22, 2014, http://www.fona.com/resource-center/blog/purchasing-power-women.

19. Benko and Pelster, "How Women Decide" *Harvard Business Review*, September 2013.

20. Pyarelal Nayyar, *Mahatma Gandhi: The Last Phase, Vol. 2* (Ahmedabad: Navajivan Publishing House, 1958) 65.

21. Tore Frängsmyr, ed., and Irwin Abrams, ed., *Nobel Lectures, Peace 1971-1980* (Singapore: World Scientific Publishing, 1997).

More Best Selling Sales & Success Books

So, You're New to Sales
By Bryan Flanagan

Bryan Flanagan wastes no time in instructing those new to the world of sales. He is direct, succinct, and uses as few words as possible to make it absolutely clear that selling is a learned skill and that professional salespeople are the ones who understand that selling is not about being a certain personality type, it is about being the go-to person, the problem solver, and the solution finder in the lives of those who need their product or service.

From start to finish, Bryan focuses on every step necessary to become a skilled professional salesperson. This work is the complete beginner "how to" book on sales. The economic climate of today is making the world of selling a viable option for many who previously never would have considered selling an option. This book makes the option of earning a living in sales viable! Read it and learn what all existing salespeople already know...a good salesperson ALWAYS has job security!

How to Stay Motivated, Volume I
An Authoritative Look at Motivation
by the World's #1 Motivator

What can you learn about motivation from the world's greatest motivator, **Zig Ziglar**? *How to Stay Motived: Developing the Qualities of Success* was created with a focus on helping people succeed. Zig had a passion for helping people become their best and this program was designed to help you grow personally and professionally in four critical areas: qualities, abilities, skills, and attitudes.

By focusing on these four core areas, you gain characteristics of success, professionalism, excellence, and perhaps the very best return of all: improved overall performance. *Developing the Qualities of Success* will cover:

1. Planning, preparing and expecting to win
2. Taking the first step to a brighter future
3. Motivation, the key to accomplishment
4. Identifying the qualities of success
5. Developing the qualities of success
6. Maintaining a winning attitude

In this valuable program, Zig encourages you to remember, "You were designed for accomplishment. You were engineered for success. You were endowed with the seeds of greatness." Apply these winning steps from the motivational master himself to build a better, more productive and satisfying life for yourself and what you do for yourself will naturally extend to your family. Developing the qualities of success will help you maintain your motivation, through all the ups and downs of life. Join millions who have used the success principles from Zig Ziglar and we will see you at the top!

Sales Success
By Zig Ziglar, Tom Hopkins, Scott McKain and more

Can a book actually help you close more sales? Yes it can! *Sales Success* is the book that shapes sales careers. While reading this sales fable, learn sales strategies used and recommended by members of the sales hall of fame including Zig Ziglar, Tom Hopkins and Scott McKain. In *Sales Success*, you will discover why sales success happens for the earnest student...and why it doesn't for the rest.

Come along with master storyteller, Mark Bowser, as he takes you on a journey of discovering ultimate sales success. You will meet Digger Jones, the mentor we all wished we had. Follow along as Digger teaches, motivates, and inspires his young protégé from failure to the heights of sales achievement...and learn how you can apply these lessons to your own sales journey.

Make a Fortune Selling to Women
By Connie Podesta

Want to Close The Deal? Want to Make The Sale? Want to Retain More Customers? Are you selling to the dominant economic force in the country?

There are 190 million of them in the U.S. alone. They have $4.4 trillion in collective buying power. They purchase 85% of all products and services, and they influence most of the rest of the purchases. They are responsible for 85% of the checks written. Forty-seven percent of them are stockholders. Who are they? Women.

In *Make a Fortune Selling to Women,* **Connie Podesta** combines psychology and sales tactics to create a how-to guide for how to sell to women and how to market to women.

With a lively voice and no-nonsense tone that both men and women will appreciate, Podesta offers specific tips for overcoming the big five Deal Breakers:

1. She doesn't want to play the game
2. She doesn't think the salesperson views her as a legitimate decision maker
3. She doesn't like the salesperson
4. She doesn't trust the salesperson
5. She doesn't think the salesperson is the right person for the job

Riddled with revealing anecdotes, *Make a Fortune Selling to Women* describes the male and female approach to the buying experience—without being condescending to either gender. And both salesmen and saleswomen will rely on this book to help them secure more sales with women. Discover exactly the right approach when selling to women and use it to close the deal.

CPSIA information can be obtained
at www.ICGtesting.com
Printed in the USA
BVOW04s1628260217
477181BV00002B/2/P